DO NOT REMOVE
CARDS FROM POCKET

AMERICAN
IMMIGRATION
TODAY

Pressures,
Problems,
Policies

AMERICAN
IMMIGRATION
TODAY
Pressures,
Problems,
Policies

Judith Bentley

Julian Messner
New York

Copyright © 1981 by Judith Bentley.

Manufactured in the United States of America.

Design by Irving Perkins Associates

Photos: Wide World

Library of Congress Cataloging in Publication Data

Bentley, Judith.
    American immigration today.

    Bibliography: p.
    Includes index.
    Summary: Discusses patterns of immigration into the United States and the ethical, political, and economic issues related to American immigration laws and policies.
    1. United States—Emigration and immigration.
    [1. United States—Emigration and immigration]
    I. Title.
    JV6455.B46   304.8′73   81-11136
    ISBN 0-671-34056-5   AACR2

Frontispiece: Three young Korean girls with the federal judge who presided at the naturalization ceremony in which they became United States citizens in Washington, D.C., in 1976.

2167869

CONTENTS

To Sheila Lawrence and Norma Rivers,
without whom I could not work

AMERICAN IMMIGRATION TODAY

Pressures, Problems, Policies

Chapter I
THE NEWEST IMMIGRANTS

Remember, remember always, that all of us . . .
are descended from immigrants.

FERNANDO MARTINEZ, a Cuban, quickly boarded a plane to Miami twenty-one years ago when a friend in Castro's government told him he was about to be arrested. Six months later, in February 1961, he volunteered to take part in the Bay of Pigs invasion attempt, after which he spent a year in jail in Cuba before he was able to return to the United States. Now he is here to stay: citizen, banker, father of two teenage sons who were born here. His sons consider themselves American, but they know they are Cuban, too. "To me it would be a disgrace if they couldn't speak Spanish," Martinez said. In addition to being a success by American standards, he values his Cuban identity.

ERLINDA NOOL decided to study nursing in the Philippines just so she would be given preference in immigrating to the United States. After finishing school she worked in hospitals, first in Manila and then in Montreal, where she was recruited by the director of Brooklyn Hospital, which needed registered nurses. She has been living and working in Brooklyn since 1971, returning to the Philippines briefly to marry her fiancé, who now works here as a salesman. Ms. Nool became a citizen in 1976 so she could bring her mother here. Her mother will stay only long enough to bring her other two daughters through. (A provision in U. S. immigration law gives preference to unmarried sons and daughters of legal immigrants.) Ms. Nool is part of the brain drain—the migration of the skilled and educated from the Third World to the highly developed countries. Why did she come? "To earn more money. You hear about everyone have cars and everything."

NORMA BECKLES Rivers came to New York City in 1972 on a one-year tourist visa. She left her two children in their grandmother's care in Barbados, took a job as a live-in housekeeper, and stayed on after her visa expired. While going through the process of certification as a needed employee, she married an American citizen and automatically became "legal." Her children have now joined her, and she has attended a community college nights to complete a secretarial course. Her reasons for coming? She was encouraged by her sister, who was already here and told her she would be able to "do more for my kids and maybe do more for myself because there's a whole lot of opportunity here. . . . I had this thing in my head about coming to America." She thought, "When I get here, I got it made. . . . People come back with such great tales." She found they were not all true.

MARTINEZ, NOOL, RIVERS—refugee, immigrant professional, economic exile—are among the newest immigrants to the United States. Most such immigrants have come since 1965, the year amendments to the immigration law changed U. S. policy and changed the very identity of those who would come. In general, the amendments made admission equally available to all nationalities and gave no preferences to any ethnic groups. Among the newest immigrants are many Asians, speakers of Spanish, political refugees, relatives of those already here, and temporary migrants who plan to return home as soon as they make enough money. Many are also coming or staying illegally. Both kinds of immigration, legal and illegal, are heavier now than they have been in more than half a century.

In 1965 Congress eliminated national-origins quotas, changing a policy that had been in effect for forty years. Since 1921 immigration into the United States had been limited by quotas for different nations. The quotas were set according to the ethnic makeup of the United States in the 1920s. Northern and western Europeans, including British, Dutch, Germans, and Scandinavians, were welcomed into the country; those from southern and eastern Europe—Italians, Slavs, Poles, Greeks—were not. Few Africans were interested in coming; their ancestors had been forced to emigrate centuries before. Chinese and most other Asians were completely excluded. No quotas at all were placed on people from Western Hemisphere countries: any number of people could immigrate from Canada, Mexico, the Caribbean, Central and South America.

Despite the nationality restrictions, the traditional American ideal has been to extend open arms to the oppressed of the world. George Washington said that the "bosom of America is open to receive not only the opulent and respectable stranger, but the oppressed and persecuted of all nations and religions." Emma Lazarus repeated this in "The New Colossus," the poem that was inscribed on the base of the Statue of Liberty in 1866: "Give me your tired, your poor,/Your huddled masses yearning to breathe free,/The wretched refuse of your teeming shore,/Send these, the homeless, tempest-tossed, to me:/I lift my lamp beside the golden door."

For its first hundred years, the nation needed immigrants. There were vast, sparsely populated acres to fill, forests to clear, land to cultivate, a native people—the Indians—to conquer, and later railroads to build, factories to run, and cities to develop. Those who immigrated were not always the elite. Fidel Castro was not the first to empty his jails by sending the inmates abroad. All who could muster the price of crossing the Atlantic or hire themselves out in advance for the price of passage could come. Almost 50 million did, from 1789 to 1980; 85 percent of them were from Europe and Canada.

They came for many reasons: economic, political, and personal. By and large they were a shade more ambitious and adventuresome than their fellows who stayed at home. They usually had a strong desire to better themselves, to come up in the world. Sometimes they had no choice. More than 1½ million Irish, for instance, were on the brink of starvation when they left home, after blight destroyed the potato crop for four consecutive years. Immigrants today give the same reasons for coming as their predecessors did. Many are still pushed by near-starvation.

Thus was established the reputation of the United States as a nation of immigrants, as echoed in the title of a book by John F. Kennedy. Franklin D. Roosevelt had said it, too: "Remember, remember always, that all of us ... are descended from immigrants."

But there were times when Americans resented the "huddled masses" and did not want to welcome any more poor people. These people competed for jobs, worked for lower wages, and sold goods at lower prices. There has been a dual tradition: of open arms on the one hand and a fear of foreigners on the other. This ambivalence in attitudes surfaced after the middle of the nineteenth century, when the country began to fill up with people. Senator John Davies of Massachusetts expressed the resentment as early as 1836: "Now sir, is it just? . . . Is it morally right for Great Britain to attempt to throw upon us this oppressive burden of sustaining her poor?" In response to these fears and resentments, the United States first began controlling immigration in 1875.

The first restrictions on immigrants were qualitative; they attempted to control the kind of individuals who would or would not be admitted. The 1875 federal law excluded convicts (but not those convicted of political offenses) and prostitutes. In 1882 lunatics, idiots, and persons likely to become public charges were excluded. By 1907 the list included polygamists, those convicted of crimes of moral turpitude (depravity), paupers, those afflicted with a dangerous disease, the insane, epileptics, professional beggars, and political radicals such as anarchists. These laws had little practical effect, however. Between 1900 and 1910 only 1¼ percent of immigrants were rejected.

Besides defining undesirables, one early law—the Chinese Exclusion Act of 1882—was aimed at a particular national group. The Chinese had not come through what Emma Lazarus described as the "golden door" of New York harbor. They had come instead to the "mountain of gold"—the hills of San Francisco during the days of the Gold Rush. They came to mine, to build the railroads, and to labor on the sugarcane plantations of Hawaii. Once the railroads were built, the Chinese were seen as competitors with native workers and as strikebreakers against emerging unions. Native workers began to urge that foreign laborers be excluded. The Chinese Exclusion Act suspended the immigration of Chinese laborers for the next sixty years.

The Chinese were seen primarily as economic rather

than political immigrants. They were not coming to seek freedom but to escape extreme poverty and support their families in China. Because of the large Chinese population, many Americans on the West Coast feared that the Chinese might overrun California. After the Hearst newspapers began a campaign against what was labeled the "yellow peril," virtually all immigration from Asia was banned in 1917.

On the East Coast, at the turn of the century, "new immigrants" were coming from southern and eastern Europe. The number of "old immigrants" from 1840 to 1880 had averaged about 250,000 a year. But between 1900 and 1910 nearly nine million newcomers arrived, and native-born Americans were made uneasy by the new nationalities— Poles, Slavs, Italians, Russians, and Greeks. The new groups were considered culturally different, inexperienced in democracy, and of a different social class—peasants and the urban lower class. The dominant ethnic group in America by 1900 was white Anglo-Saxon Protestant; the new immigrants were Catholic or Jewish and not Anglo-Saxon.

Another reason the new immigrants were disliked was that they seemed to settle in groups. Woodrow Wilson stated in 1915 that this was not acceptable: "America does not consist of groups. A man who thinks of himself as belonging to a particular national group in America has not yet become an American."

The solution was for the immigrants to assimilate, to become as much like the natives as they could—in dress, speech, food preference, and life-style. Ideally, to assimilate, they should give up their own cultures and languages and become "100 percent American," a popular phrase in the 1920s. During World War I, Germans came under heavy pressure to give up their German-language schools, newspapers, and so-

nedy. The national-origins quotas, opposed by many in the 1950s, seemed even more objectionable in the 1960s, when Congress was passing major civil rights legislation. Amendments abolishing the quotas were completed in 1965 and signed into law by President Lyndon Johnson.

In place of the quotas, the 1965 amendments instituted a complex preference system for countries in the Eastern Hemisphere. The system gives preference to immigrants with relatives already in the United States and immigrants who have talents and skills that are needed here. Every country in the Eastern Hemisphere—including Asian and African countries—was given the same limit: 20,000 immigrants a year. A ceiling of 170,000 was set for immigrants from the Eastern Hemisphere and 120,000 for those from the Western Hemisphere. The preference system and per-country limits were not extended to Western Hemisphere countries until 1976. And until that year there was no special method for allocating the 120,000 visas available to Western Hemisphere residents.

The 1965 amendments marked the first time a ceiling had been set on Western Hemisphere immigration. It was added at the last minute as part of a trade-off for abolishing the national-origins quotas. Senator Sam Ervin insisted on the ceiling because "everybody from the Western Hemisphere might suddenly decide to move to the United States and thus flood our country with immigrants we could not assimilate for many generations." In fact, Western Hemisphere immigration had been increasing, and the majority in Congress feared a massive increase in Latin Americans, including blacks.

The new system was phased in after June 30, 1968. By 1980 the total worldwide ceiling had been increased to 290,000, plus 50,000 refugees a year. Despite this ceiling, more than 800,000 immigrants were admitted legally in 1980, including some 151,000 not subject to numerical limits and 367,000 refugees and special entrants.

Preference System (1965 Amendments to Immigration and Nationality Act of 1952)

FIRST	Unmarried sons and daughters, twenty-one years of age or older, of U. S. citizens (20 percent).
SECOND	Husbands, wives, and unmarried sons and daughters of permanent resident aliens (20 percent).
THIRD	Professionals and people of exceptional ability in the sciences and arts who will benefit the economy, culture, or welfare of the United States (10 percent).
FOURTH	Married children of U. S. citizens (10 percent).
FIFTH	Brothers and sisters, twenty-one years of age or older, of U. S. citizens (24 percent).
SIXTH	Skilled or unskilled workers needed in the U. S. labor market who will not displace citizens or legal alien workers (10 percent).
*SEVENTH	Refugees from communist or communist-dominated countries, the Middle East, or areas struck by natural disaster (6 percent).

SOURCE: The Select Commission on Immigration and Refugee Policy
* Replaced by Refugee Act of 1980

A preference system is used to determine which 20,000 Filipinos, for example, may immigrate each year (see table). Certain kinds of immigrants are not included in the limit. They are spouses, children, and parents of adult U. S. citizens, ministers of religion and their families (an exemption that is intended to ensure freedom of religion), and certain employees or former employees of the U. S. government abroad and their families. (This explains the 200,000 immigrants who entered outside the ceiling in 1978.)

Within the 20,000 limit, an immigrant may qualify for a

visa in any one of seven different categories. In those categories 74 percent of the slots are available to relatives of U. S. citizens and permanent resident aliens (immigrants who have been legally admitted but are not yet citizens). The relatives may be unmarried adult sons and daughters of citizens; spouses and unmarried sons and daughters of permanent residents; or married children, or brothers and sisters of citizens. The remaining 26 percent of the slots are for professionals, scientists, artists of exceptional ability, skilled and unskilled workers in occupations for which there is a labor shortage in the United States, and refugees. (Refugees were removed from the preference system in 1980.)

A prospective immigrant must obtain an immigrant visa from the U. S. consulate in his or her country. Visas are distributed within each preference category on a first-come, first-served basis. If there aren't enough brothers and sisters of citizens who want to emigrate, the remaining numbers in that category may be given to another category. Some countries, such as Switzerland and Austria, seldom use more than a few hundred visas. In other countries, such as the Philippines, a prospective immigrant may have to wait as long as ten years before a slot is available. Since per-country limits were applied to the Western Hemisphere in 1976 the backlog of Latin Americans waiting for visas has been steadily increasing.

Less significant changes have been made since 1965, but the major shift in U. S. policy was the abolition of differential national quotas. Before looking at the results of this shift, let us examine what has been happening in the world to create the immigration pressures on our borders.

Global Movements

People have always migrated, leaving the familiar in search of something better, but migration is occurring in even greater numbers today than it did in the past. It has become much easier to see the greener grass on the other side of the border—the better job, the higher wages, the superior educational system. The individual decisions of a Pakistani to work in Iran, an Indian medical student to seek further training in the United States, a Salvadorean peasant to move next door to Honduras to find farmland, a Mexican worker to return to his family are multiplied a thousandfold every year, creating a constant flux of migrants.

The flow of migrants in mid-twentieth century is most often from developing Third World countries to the developed countries, from rural to urban, and from former colonies to former colonial powers. Emigration from Europe to new colonies and countries has declined, and migration from poorer countries in Asia, Africa, and Latin America has boomed.

In the past, immigration has been beneficial to both the sending and receiving countries. It helped to relieve population pressures in the sending countries and contributed to the development of the receiving countries. But today not many countries need people or have land left to settle. Only a very few, like Argentina, still encourage immigration.

People become immigrants today largely because they are "pushed" out of their own countries. Demographers talk about push-pull factors, the reasons people feel forced to leave one country and are attracted to another. One of the biggest pushes comes from population growth. The world population will increase another 50 percent by 1990. The populations of Mexico and many of the Caribbean countries will more than double in our lifetime. As populations increase, resources dwindle. These countries will not have enough land, jobs, or even food to go around. Since the world's wealth, especially the food supply, is unevenly distributed, many people will emigrate in order to survive.

An example of what can happen as the result of extreme population pressures was the so-called Soccer War between Honduras and El Salvador in 1969. Both countries are extremely poor, but El Salvador has more people to share the poverty—about 400 per square mile. In the years before 1969, almost 10 percent of the Salvadorean population had moved into neighboring Honduras in search of land for subsistence farming. At first the Hondurans accepted the Salvadoreans, but when big Honduran farmers and ranchers wanted more land to raise beef and cotton for export, they blamed the "foreigners" for land invasions. After a World Cup regional soccer match, which Honduras lost to El Salvador, Honduras decided to expel the Salvadoreans. The Salvadorean army went to the border to prevent the peasants from returning and then invaded. After three days a cease-fire was arranged. The Organization of American States gave the cause of the brief war as "population pressure."

El Salvador's population continues to increase at a rate that will double its size in twenty years. More and more Salvadoreans are now making their way across Mexico to the U. S. border.

Unemployment is another push factor. The World Bank estimated in the mid-1970s that there was 15 percent unemployment in Mexico, 17 percent in the Dominican Republic, 20 percent in El Salvador, and 15 percent in Guatemala.

When underemployment is included, the rates increase to 15–30 percent for Mexico, 60 percent in the Dominican Republic, 30–50 percent for El Salvador, 40 percent for Brazil, and 17–30 percent in Colombia.

Other push factors include compulsory military service, as in Greece. Crop failures or years of scarcity can spur an exodus of people, as they did for Cubans in the spring of 1980. Political instability or a feeling that violence is about to occur can also push people to leave.

Immigrants do not usually come from the poorest countries in the world. People who are extremely poor don't know where to go and don't have the money to travel anywhere. Immigrants tend to be people who have glimpsed a better life. They come from countries in which there has been rapid economic expansion that has led to higher expectations. The expansion may benefit only the elite, however, and do little to improve the living standards of the masses, who leave the rural areas and come to the cities to find work. Or a country may begin to educate more people but then be unable to provide jobs for them. When expectations of a better life are not met, people begin to look around for another opportunity.

The opportunity comes from jobs—the pull factors—in more developed countries. There is also the pull of abundant food, consumer goods, and the attractions of American pop culture—Levis, Coke, Western music. Letters from those who have already come magnify the attractions.

Jobs are available in the industrialized countries, even during recessions and times of high unemployment. They are the jobs native workers consider undesirable, because they are monotonous, backbreaking, bad-smelling, dirty, or low-paying jobs as dishwashers, day laborers, street cleaners, janitors and custodians, parking lot attendants, fruit and vegetable packers, baggage handlers, truck and gypsy cab drivers, servants, and baby-sitters.

A growing number of economic exiles are happy to have these jobs. They will cross national borders or wander from city to city, looking for a way to survive and make enough money to return home. They have become an international labor reserve that countries like Switzerland, France, Germany, and the United States use when they need cheap labor.

Much of the movement of economic exiles across borders is illegal. Countries with intense pressures for emigration and waiting lists for visas are prime sources of illegal immigrants to the United States. Some of these countries are Mexico, Jamaica, the Dominican Republic, Haiti, Korea, the Philippines, Thailand, and China. The risk involved in illegal immigration is slight; once the immigrants arrive here, they probably won't be found and deported.

A different type of international migration is the so-called brain drain—the movement of the talented and educated to the developed countries. This professional elite is attracted by better jobs, advanced education and training, more research facilities, higher wages, and higher social status. Many graduates of India's schools and universities, for example, end up unemployed or underemployed in India. The Republic of the Philippines educates large numbers of doctors and nurses but is unable to keep them at home.

Immigrants Admitted by Country or Region of Birth
(Years Ended June 30, 1976, and June 30, 1965)

COUNTRY OF BIRTH	NUMBER 1976	1965	PERCENT CHANGE
All countries	398,613	296,697	+34.4
Europe	72,404	113,424	−36.2
Austria	344	1,680	−79.5
Belgium	386	1,005	−61.6

Immigrants Admitted by Country or Region of Birth
(Years Ended June 30, 1976, and June 30, 1965)

COUNTRY OF BIRTH	NUMBER 1976	1965	PERCENT CHANGE
Czechoslovakia	551	1,894	−70.9
Denmark	408	1,384	−70.5
France	1,478	4,039	−63.4
Germany	5,836	24,045	−75.7
Greece	8,417	3,002	+180.4
Hungary	861	1,574	−45.3
Ireland	1,171	5,463	−78.6
Italy	8,380	10,821	−22.6
Netherlands	936	3,085	−69.7
Norway	286	2,256	−87.3
Poland	3,805	8,465	−55.0
Portugal	10,511	2,005	+424.2
Romania	2,179	1,644	+32.5
Spain	2,254	2,200	+2.5
Sweden	544	2,411	−77.4
Switzerland	597	1,984	−69.9
U.S.S.R.	8,220	1,853	+343.6
United Kingdom	11,392	27,358	−58.4
Yugoslavia	2,820	2,818	+.1
Other Europe	1,028	2,438	−57.8
Asia	149,881	20,683	+624.7
China and Taiwan	18,823	4,057	+364.0
Hong Kong	5,766	712	+709.8
India	17,487	582	+2,904.6
Iran	2,700	804	+235.8
Japan	4,258	3,180	+33.9
Korea	30,803	2,165	+1,322.8
Pakistan	2,888	187	+1,444.4
Philippines	37,281	3,130	+1,091.1
Thailand	6,923	214	+3,135.0
Vietnam	3,048	226	+1,248.7
Other Asia	119,904	5,426	+266.8

Immigrants Admitted by Country or Region of Birth
(Years Ended June 30, 1976, and June 30, 1965)

COUNTRY OF BIRTH	NUMBER 1976	NUMBER 1965	PERCENT CHANGE
North America	142,307	126,729	+12.3
Canada	7,638	38,327	−80.1
Mexico	57,863	37,969	+52.4
West Indies	66,839	37,583	+77.8
Cuba	29,233	19,760	+47.9
Dominican Republic	12,526	9,504	+31.8
Haiti	5,410	3,609	+49.9
Jamaica	9,026	1,837	+391.3
Trinidad and Tobago	4,839	485	+897.7
Other West Indies	5,805	2,388	+143.1
Other North America	9,967	12,850	−22.4
South America	22,706	30,962	−26.7
Argentina	2,267	6,124	−63.0
Brazil	1,038	2,869	−63.8
Colombia	5,742	10,885	−47.3
Other South America	13,659	11,084	+23.2
Africa	7,723	3,383	+128.3
Oceania	3,591	1,512	+137.5
Other countries	1	4	−75.0

SOURCE: 1976 Annual Report of the Immigration and Naturalization Service

Sending countries may suffer from the emigration of skilled, productive young adults. More dependents are left behind—children, the aged, the emotionally, mentally, or physically disabled. But emigration can be advantageous, too; it can act as a safety valve to relieve pressure built up by intolerable conditions. Most countries don't try to keep people from leaving. "Ours is a migratory people," said an aide to the Jamaican prime minister, "and we would have a severe domestic problem if we tried to restrict their leaving."

People have an internationally recognized right to emigrate. The United Nations Universal Declaration on Human Rights states that "Everyone has the right to leave any country, including his own, and to return to his country." There is no way to guarantee the right of immigration into another country, however, and therein lies the difficulty.

Recent examples of exiles with no place to go were the boat people—the Vietnamese who were forced to emigrate with no destination that guaranteed admittance. No one country could accommodate them all, and they could not return to Vietnam. According to the United States Committee for Refugees there are currently 16 million refugees of all nationalities adrift in the world, including the Palestinians who have had no permanent home for more than thirty years.

The global picture, then, is one of rapidly increasing populations, diminishing resources, unemployment, and a large opportunity gap that encourages migration. Experts warn that the real immigration problem is only beginning. "The developed countries lie directly in the path of a great storm from the Third World," claimed a 1980 *Time* essay.

U. S. Immigration Policy Since 1965

The intent of the 1965 change in U. S. immigration law was to limit the number of immigrants but to allow people of all countries an equal opportunity to come. What has been the result of that legislation? Has it been adequate to cope with migration pressures on our borders?

There have been two major results:

1. Immigration to the United States has increased greatly, by 35 percent over the decade prior to 1965. In the early 1960s, the average annual figure was less than 300,000; in the late 1970s and early 1980s it was 400,000 to 700,000. If illegal immigration is added to this, an estimated one million people have come each year in the past decade.

2. Different nationalities are coming: more Asians and Latin Americans and fewer Europeans. In 1975 three Asians were immigrating for every two Europeans, a reversal of the 1969 ratio. In the late 1970s, some 60 percent of all legal immigrants came from nine countries: Mexico, Vietnam, the Philippines, Korea, Cuba, China and Taiwan, India, the Dominican Republic, and Jamaica.

Opening the door to all nationalities has created backlogs in some countries such as the Philippines, China, India, and Korea. The preference system has influenced the kinds of people who are admitted: the largest number are relatives of those who are already here. Coming illegally or as a relative has become the only way for the poor and working classes to immigrate. Few have been able to obtain labor certification.

Professionals, technicians, and artists find admission easier, and they constitute a larger proportion of the newest immigrants. In the decade 1901 to 1910, some 26 percent of immigrants were laborers and only 1 percent were professionals or technicians. In the decade 1961 to 1970, fewer than 4 percent were laborers and 10 percent were professionals.

Refugees have been admitted in larger numbers than was expected in 1965. The newest waves of immigrants also contain more women.

Two-thirds of the newcomers have settled in just six states: New York, California, New Jersey, Illinois, Texas, and Massachusetts. They tend to cluster on the borders and seacoasts, but they have made it to the heartland, too—the Vietnamese to Iowa, Muslims to Michigan, Mexicans to Chicago.

Today's immigrants differ from pre-1965 groups in their attitudes toward the United States. Not all rush to citizenship. Since air travel makes their homes relatively accessible, they are able to maintain personal and cultural ties. Many see this country as a good place to make money, but they are intensely aware of the cultural sacrifices they may have to make if they remain.

The newcomers have much in common with American minorities. The reaction to them is seldom openly racist, but Americans do fear being culturally overrun. The mood of the country is more cautious and less expansive than it was a century or even thirty years ago. There is an awareness of poverty, of the potential for further racial strife, of competition for jobs, and of the limits to American resources. Immigration complicates each of these problems.

As Cubans, Vietnamese, Mexicans, Haitians, and many others came ashore and across the border by the thousands in the late 1970s, a feeling developed that U. S. immigration policy was, once again, inadequate. Immigration was seen as one of the most serious problems facing the country in the decade of the 1980s. A Select Commission on Immigration and Refugee Policy, composed of members of Congress, members of the cabinet, and private citizens, was established in 1978 to make recommendations for change. The concept of a nation of immigrants was to be examined once more.

Chapter II

THE HISPANICS

So far from God and so close to the United States.

HISPANICS AND Asians predominate among the newest immigrants, far outnumbering Europeans. Of the two groups, Hispanic immigrants have the firmer toehold in the United States. They join a minority that numbers more than 12 million and will soon surpass blacks as the country's largest. Part of this increase is due to a slightly higher birthrate and a younger median age, but much of the increase comes from immigration.

Hispanic immigration is a phenomenon of the middle and late twentieth century. There have always been Mexicans in the Southwest; Puerto Ricans and Cubans have moved to and from the United States rather freely. But by 1976 Hispanics from other countries as well had boosted the total to about one-third of all newcomers. They are the largest group of immigrants who speak basically the same language. "Hispanic," in fact, is an umbrella term used to describe people of

33

twenty-three different nationalities, all of whom speak Spanish: Puerto Ricans, Cubans, Mexicans, Dominicans, Ecuadoreans, Salvadoreans, Colombians, and several other groups. The word "Hispanic" implies a historical and cultural link with Spain, but it describes the descendants of Incas and Africans as well as of Spaniards, all of whom intermingled.

As a result of immigration, the United States is now the fourth largest Spanish-speaking nation in the world. Los Angeles is the city with the largest Mexican population, after Mexico City itself, with more than a million residents of Mexican ancestry. California has 4 million Hispanics; Texas, 3 million; and New York, 2 to 2.5 million. One-fourth of U. S. Catholics are Spanish-speakers.

The impact of Hispanic immigration comes not just from numbers but from cultural strength. Hispanics are determined to retain their culture, especially their language. A 1976 survey by the U. S. Census Bureau found that four out of five Hispanics live in homes in which Spanish is spoken. One-third speak primarily Spanish. "We still maintain and speak Spanish despite the second- and third-generation youths," commented a forty-seven-year-old woman born in New York of Puerto Rican parents. "No other cultures preserve that here. It's a sore point because they say we want to be different. To this I say, 'Vive la difference!' "

Hispanics are equally determined not to let their values be subsumed. Among these are family unity; an attitude of respect toward religious, parental, and governmental authority; and warmth and compassion for one's fellow humans. "To be Hispanic," Margaret Mead said, "is to be a member of a family"—a family that extends widely over several generations and includes grandparents, aunts, uncles, cousins, and nieces. Family unity may be valued even above economic advancement. "The concept of the united family is our contribution ... to this country," commented one Hispanic.

Hispanics also perceive Americans as cold and competitive instead of humanistic. A Colombian doctor commented, "They don't care about their fellow man. ... They care only for *el numero uno*. Other people are not important." Members of one Cuban family described themselves, in contrast, as very sociable, group-oriented people having too much fun to change.

Hispanics differ from previous immigrant groups in that many do not intend to become citizens. In a *New York Times* survey, 80 percent were unwilling to call themselves Americans. "There are two sides to me, and I am still a Dominican at heart," said one respondent. "I have been here almost twenty years, but I cannot forget where I came from."

Many see their stay as temporary. Mexicans who cross the border stay an average of only six to eight months. Many others are "commuters" who cross each day to work. Some Central and South Americans stay only long enough to make money to improve their standard of living when they return or to wait out a political crisis.

Much of the Hispanic migration to the United States is illegal. Undocumented Dominicans, Colombians, and Ecuadoreans find employment easily in restaurants, hotels, and garment factories in the cities. Mexicans find employment as farm workers and as maids and child-care workers in private homes.

The status of Hispanics in the United States is generally low, although early immigrants from Colombia, Cuba, and Nicaragua were from the upper and middle classes. The median family income of families of Spanish origin was $11,420 in 1977, compared with $16,010 for the overall population.

One in four Spanish-origin families lives below the poverty level.

Part of their low status they attribute to discrimination. To Hispanics, skin color has traditionally been less important than it seems to U. S. citizens. Because of broad mixing, skin color among Spanish-speakers ranges from white to black, even within one family. But the combination of language, color, and culture sets them apart as a minority in the United States. When asked, "Is there anything in particular that has prevented you from doing all that you wanted or hoped?" a Colombian resident of the United States for twenty years responded, "Being Hispanic." Cubans seem to have suffered the least discrimination and to have prospered accordingly.

Although Hispanics are linked by language, religion, and culture, members of various nationalities differ in their reasons for being here, their legal status, their economic and social backgrounds, and their attitudes toward the United States. A more detailed look at the major groups—Mexicans, Caribbean Hispanics, Central and South Americans—will illustrate these differences.

Mexicans

Mexicans are not newcomers to the United States. Their Indian ancestors lived in the Southwest for centuries, and their Spanish forebears were the first Europeans in North America. Spaniards traveled north from Mexico four hundred years ago; Francisco Coronado, the explorer, was in Kansas in 1542, and Los Angeles was founded by forty-four Mexican immigrants in 1781. The movement north from Mexico, and usually back south again, has never really stopped.

In fact, the establishment of the U.S.-Mexican border is a fairly recent historical event. The border was set after the Mexican-American War of 1846 forced Mexico to cede most of the Southwest to the United States. The Treaty of Guadalupe Hidalgo used the Rio Grande as the dividing line in the east and then extended the line west to the ocean. At that time, 75,000 Mexicans were living in what is now mostly New Mexico and California. They had the choice of leaving within a year or staying and gaining full American citizenship.

Large numbers of Mexicans have entered and left the Southwest since then, in response to political upheavals and the need for workers in this country. More than a million left Mexico during the 1910–1920 revolution. During both world wars the United States needed laborers to maintain railroads and work in the fields. In 1942 the U. S. government established a program with Mexico to import *braceros*—workers—as they were needed. The program continued after the war, and tens of thousands of braceros came. Under pressure from American labor unions, the program was officially ended in 1964 and 200,000 Mexicans were expelled. But because the growers still wanted a temporary, flexible, cheap supply of labor, Mexicans continued to cross the border to work—this time illegally.

The typical Mexican migrant of today is much like his predecessors. He is a young, humble, frugal family man who comes looking for work and sends money home to his family. He stays only about six months. If he stays as long as five years, he returns home four or five times during that period, usually for holidays.

Another migrant may live with her family near the border and commute daily to the nearby cities of El Paso, San Diego, or Brownsville, Texas, to work as a maid or baby-sitter. Most have no plans to immigrate, although many stay far longer than they had originally planned or make several trips to the United States in a lifetime.

Overall, Mexico sends more immigrants, both legal and illegal, than any other country. Before the 20,000 limit was extended to Western Hemisphere countries, legal immigration from Mexico had reached 70,000 in 1974. Imposition of the limit created a backlog and spurred an unknown number of illegal migrants. The Immigration and Naturalization Service (INS) apprehended a million illegal Mexican aliens in 1979. (But this figure does not represent a million different people. The same migrant may be caught more than once.) A 1980 Census Bureau study concluded that there are "almost certainly" fewer than three million illegal Mexicans now in the United States, "possibly only 1.5 to 2.5 million." Enough is known of the numbers, however, to confirm that Mexicans outnumber peoples of any other nationality who come here.

As a result of years of immigration, Mexican-Americans now constitute the second largest minority in this country and 59 percent of its Hispanics. More than 7 million people of Mexican origin were living here in 1979, most in the Southwest. They account for about 40 percent of the population in New Mexico, 19 percent in Arizona, 18 percent in Texas, 16 percent in California, and 13 percent in Colorado.

Among those who stay in the United States, the urge to keep their language, traditions, and Mexican citizenship is strong. To give up their heritage would be considered unpatriotic, like "stepping on the Mexican flag." Whereas about one-third of all immigrants between 1966 and 1970 chose to become citizens in the following five years, only one-eighth of Mexicans did.

If Mexicans do not long to be a part of the total American dream, why do they come? Most come to feed their families. Mexico has too many people and not enough jobs. Until 1972, when the Mexican government started an intensive family-planning effort, Mexico's population was the fastest growing in the world, among large countries. By the year 2000 Mexico is expected to have at least 110 million people, a tenfold increase in a hundred years.

Mexico has also had the highest economic development of any Latin American country in the 1960s and 1970s, but the benefits of that development have not yet filtered down to the poor. With the discovery of huge deposits of oil, Mexico may become the world's first- or second-largest oil producer by the year 2000, and this is bound to spur economic development further.

In the meantime the situation is critical. Unemployment in 1975 was officially estimated at nearly 50 percent. Rural peasants have been particularly hard hit by insufficient crops, erosion, aridity, the general exhaustion of the soil, and the problem of finding markets for their products. Even in the cities, wages are never more than about one-third of the minimum wage on this side of the border. This has spurred migration to the cities and to the United States. About one in seven Mexican workers has come to the United States illegally at some point in order to earn a living.

Nowhere else in the world does such a flimsy border separate a large, poor, underdeveloped country from a large, rich, overdeveloped one. The border has been called one of the most unrealistic in the Western Hemisphere. It has few natural barriers: desert, a narrow shallow river, and an occasional fence. Nor is it a strong psychological barrier because of the shared people, history, economy, and traditions. Yet it does separate the rich and the poor, and that gap encourages migration. The Mexicans have a saying: "So far from God and so close to the United States."

Transporting Mexicans across the border is becoming a flourishing business in border cities such as Tijuana, across from San Diego, and Juarez, across from El Paso. Job seekers from the interior arrive in trucks and buses, their passage arranged by "coyotes"—smugglers. The coyotes may offer a package deal to the United States: border crossing and transportation to a job, for a fee. Taxi companies and mini-buses offer transportation to Chicago, San Francisco, Denver, and Dallas.

Many Mexicans also live in border towns and commute across the border daily to work. Thirteen thousand in the Juarez–El Paso area have permanent resident alien cards that allow them to cross the border legally. Thousands of young women come to work as housemaids and baby-sitters, earning as little as $25 a week. An estimated 12,000 to 20,000 live in as maids in homes in San Antonio; at least 20,000 in El Paso; and some 60,000 in Los Angeles.

The number of Mexican women coming to the United States has increased greatly in recent years. They now constitute one-third of all the illegal immigrants apprehended in large cities such as New York. Women are welcomed because of the low wages they will accept and because they are perceived as docile workers.

Mexicans who are here to stay have begun the long process of accommodating to American life and of making themselves known, accepted, and even appreciated. Unlike some earlier immigrant groups, Mexican newcomers must combat a historically disadvantageous position in American society. They face a legacy of hostility in the Southwest that has survived since the Battle of the Alamo, when Mexican General Santa Anna and 5,000 soldiers killed all 183 defenders of the Texas fort in 1836. "To this day the Alamo remains a symbol in the American mind of the Mexican as a cruel bar-

barian and part of the excuse for a much more enduring barbarism toward Mexicans on the part of the Anglos," write the authors of *The Golden Door.* The 1970 U. S. Commission on Civil Rights reported that in five southwestern states Mexican-American citizens are subject to harsh treatment by law officers, arrested for little reason, given disproportionately severe penalties, and subjected to physical and verbal abuse and even death at the hands of the police.

The most recent image of Mexican-Americans has been shaped by Cesar Chavez and the farm workers. Chavez began organizing fellow Mexican-American grape pickers in the mid-1950s to demand higher wages from the California growers. By the time the strike succeeded in the mid-1970s it had attained the status of *la causa* for Mexican-Americans and had attracted nationwide attention and support for its consumer boycott of grapes.

The economic beginning also gave rise to a broader political movement among Chicanos, as some Mexican-Americans began calling themselves. Chicanos started their own political party, La Raza Unida, in Texas and began wielding political power as a voting bloc to be courted by the major parties.

Through political action, Mexican-Americans also hoped to attack other problems: their low economic status, social mobility limited by language and color, and difficulties with the schools. Economically, Mexican-Americans still constitute one-third of the people living below the poverty level in Texas and New Mexico and one-quarter of those in Arizona and Colorado. In 1975 the median income for families of Mexican origin was $9,500, compared with more than $16,000 for all families.

Economic position is often related to education, and many Mexican-Americans lack strong educational backgrounds. Until 1930 education was regarded as a luxury available only to the upper classes in Mexico. Adult illegal immigrants come here with an average of two to four years of schooling. Children who travel with their migrant parents do not fare much better. U. S. teachers and administrators were neither prepared to educate Spanish-speaking children nor particularly sympathetic to them. Mexican parents see the schools as a threat to their own authority and to the values and culture they want their children to cherish. As a result, Mexicans have not used education to advance themselves as have other immigrant groups, such as Orientals, Jews, and Germans. The drop-out rate for Mexican-Americans in the Denver schools is 80 percent, twice the rate for black students.

Mexican-Americans have also hoped to change their image. They particularly dislike the depiction of the Mexican as a dirty, ignorant, evil-smelling, mustachioed, sombreroed villain. A group in Hollywood called Justice for Chicanos in the Motion Picture and Television Industry objected to the movies *Butch Cassidy and the Sundance Kid* and *The Wild Bunch,* for example. In some motion pictures, Anglos who are vastly outnumbered consistently outgun whole armies of Mexicans and other Latin Americans—a variation on the cowboys and Indians theme.

The antagonism grows out of the close historical relationship between the two countries. The United States sees Mexico as unwilling or unable to solve its problems, which spill across the border. Mexico sees the United States as exploitative and contributing to those problems. Americans fear that too many Mexicans will crowd U. S. cities, lower wages, drain social services such as medical care and welfare, and become a burden on the schools. Mexico sees that the United States would like to buy oil at a reasonable price, continue to import cheap labor when it is needed, and keep fruit and vegetable prices low. It does not view emigration as a problem.

Some resolutions of the continuing dilemma have been suggested. One is to give Mexico a higher quota as a neighbor than the 20,000 per-country limit. Another is to reinstitute a bracero-type program and legalize the flow of workers. Any real diminution in the flow of Mexicans will depend on improvements within Mexico, which the United States may also be willing to support.

Caribbean Hispanics

CUBANS

Fernando J. Martinez, who left Cuba at age twenty, is now a vice-president of the First National Bank of Greater Miami and well established in the Miami community. Such success is not unusual for a member of the first wave of Cubans who emigrated to the United States in the early 1960s. They came as political refugees, predominantly from the middle and upper classes, and they thrived to an unusual degree.

Martinez's first job in this country was in a grocery store in Miami Beach where he worked for $45 a week. He subsequently worked in a small loan company, then as manager of a financial services company, in real estate in Puerto Rico, for banks and a builder, and eventually for First National. Thus, he worked his way up the economic ladder with help from relatives and friends, a middle-class background, and his own personality. He spoke English when he arrived because, as a child, he had attended American summer camps.

Making the short hop from Cuba to the tip of Florida has been a frequent experience for Cubans—for education, travel, summer camp, and political sanctuary. Cuba's history, like that of Mexico, is intertwined with the history of the United States. Political opponents of Caribbean dictators like Trujillo in the Dominican Republic and Batista in Cuba have frequently fled to this country to carry on their opposition from a distance or wait until it was safe to return home.

The first large exodus of Cubans was very much in this tradition. After Castro assumed power in January 1959, Cuba experienced a far-reaching social, economic, and political revolution. Because the revolution was a reaction to the U. S.-dominated Batista regime, it was only natural for the exiles to flee here. But the numbers who came and the warmth of their welcome were unusual. Since there were no restrictions on immigration from the Western Hemisphere, Cubans were free to come here and free to leave Cuba, at first.

The first to flee were the members of Batista's power structure, followed by the owners of farms, ranches, and businesses whose property had been confiscated. Then came the professionals. All these groups brought considerable money, possessions, and skills with them. As the revolution became more radical, teachers, accountants, and retail clerks, merchants, landlords, military men, and skilled laborers joined the exodus.

More than 800,000 Cubans have immigrated since the end of 1958. The United States has made it easy for them to come. They were allowed in without passports or visas, and in 1961 a federal agency was established to aid them. It spent $1.3 billion for medical and social services and for resettlement aid. Almost two-thirds of the Cubans who came before 1980 came via airlifts paid for by the U. S. government.

The flow of Cubans was advantageous to both Cuba and the United States. Politically, U. S. leaders viewed the immigration as evidence of the failure of communism, evidence that was highly visible to the world. American society also benefited from the influx of money and skilled and educated people. Castro benefited because he could rid Cuba of those who were dissatisfied with the way things were going. Clearly the exodus was facilitated by geographical nearness and the cooperation of the U. S. government. Castro commented on this policy: "Any other Latin American country to which [the United States] made such an offer would empty out overnight."

Miami was the first and permanent goal of most of the refugees. It had a warm climate like Cuba's, and 70 percent of the refugees had close friends or relatives who were already in the United States, most in Miami. It was much easier for Cubans to make an occupational adjustment in an established Cuban community that was receptive to their education and skills. Moreover, many Cubans thought they would soon be returning to Cuba; they did not want to move too far away.

Miami could not absorb all those who wanted to settle there, however, and large numbers were relocated to cities like New Orleans and Indianapolis or Weehawken, Elizabeth, Union City, or West New York, New Jersey. So many settled in Union City that it became known as Little Havana on the Hudson. Its 200,000 Cubans, plus another 250,000 in surrounding communities, make it second only to Miami's 500,000. New York City has an estimated 107,000 Cubans. As a result of the resettlement program, over half of all Cubans in the United States lived outside the greater Miami area prior to the 1980 influx.

Wherever Cubans settled, they prospered and, according to one writer, achieved "middle-class status faster than any other ethnic group since the Huguenots of colonial times." According to 1976 figures, the median family income for Cubans was $11,800, the highest among Hispanics. Cubans place a high value on education, and their children learned English quickly.

As Miami's Cubans adjusted, they transformed the city. In 1960 it was primarily a tourist town, fading in attractiveness. During the next twenty years, a process that has been dubbed the "Latinization of Miami" began. Today Miami is a booming commercial city that seems more Caribbean than North American in style. It is a regional shopping center for wealthy Latin Americans and a center for foreign banking and investments. Nearly 40 percent of Miami's population is of Latin heritage, and local officials declared Dade a bicultural-bilingual county in 1973. This means primarily that business can be conducted in either Spanish or English. Speaking both languages has become a prerequisite for many jobs.

Cubans now constitute 52 percent of the inner city of Miami and 55 percent of suburban Hialeah. They are particularly prevalent in banking, hotels, and construction. They control 40 percent of the southeast Florida construction business, make up 60 percent of the construction work force, hold most of the service jobs in restaurants, and constitute one-third of banking employees. An estimated 18,000 Miami enterprises are owned by Cubans who were thus able to provide jobs for refugees who came in the 1970s.

The political adjustment of the Cuban exile community has been much slower than the economic. The early refugees thought, as refugees often do, that they would be able to return home soon. As Castro continued to maintain a firm grip, however, they gradually began to settle into American society more fully. "We are changing from exiles to immigrants," says Miami lawyer Marino Lopez-Bianco. There is less talk of "when we return" and more of attaining middle-class status while maintaining pride in a Cuban heritage. As they have acquired citizenship, Cubans have become more powerful.

and cirrhosis of the liver (brought on by alcoholism)

erto Rican communities are well established in the
States, but they have not used political power effec-
There have been scattered individual successes: Mayor
e Ferre of Miami, Congressman Herman Badillo from
nx, and Joseph Montserrat, a past president of the
ork City Board of Education, whose students are one-
ispanic. A group called the Young Lords demon-
in the 1960s for free food and Puerto Rican studies
is, but no strong Puerto Rican political organization
lved. Ferre and other leaders have urged Puerto
to become more active in politics. "Rather than con-
ng on Puerto Rican independence, we should get
volved in the politics of this country," he said.

e lag in acculturation and economic achievement is
ue to a clash in values. Puerto Ricans value family life
pontaneous, intimate, emotive community life. They
drug addiction, organized crime, union gangsterism,
er social ills with the United States and fear they will
o the island.

rto Ricans have suffered discrimination on the main-
ecause blacks and whites have intermingled for cen-
Puerto Rico, skin color does not have the importance
at it has in the United States. Puerto Ricans identify
ves more by nationality or cultural background than
Since Puerto Ricans are Hispanics, their position in
n society influences the acculturation of other His-
migrants and the American reaction to them.

CANS

minicans, like Cubans and Puerto Ricans, are Carib-
ispanics. They come from an island the Dominican

Twenty thousand became citizens in Dade County alone in
1976, making them the county's largest voting minority.

A few still have not given up the hope of overthrowing
Castro. Terrorist groups like Omega 7 have bombed the offices of international companies that trade with Cuba; they
have threatened, harassed, and even assassinated Cuban-
Americans who are more willing to accept the situation.

A reopening of some communication between the Cuban
government and its exiles in the United States occurred during the November 1978 "dialogue" and encouraged the sudden exodus from Cuba in the spring of 1980. Cuban family
ties are strong, and many exiles had been trying for a long
time to bring relatives they had left behind. Success stories
from the United States helped strengthen the urge to emigrate.

The exodus began when more than ten thousand Cubans
crowded onto the grounds of the Peruvian embassy in Havana seeking exit visas. Castro had said that anyone who
wished to leave Cuba should go there. The embassy granted
them temporary asylum and began looking for countries to
accept them.

This action provided an opening for Cuban-Americans,
who chartered a small flotilla of pleasure and fishing boats to
bring their friends and relatives out. Three thousand boats
left the southern tip of Florida, and in just three months,
114,000 Cubans were brought in. The total eventually
reached 125,000.

This sudden rush to U. S. shores caused a new problem
in immigration policy. The immigrants were entering illegally, but once they were here it was difficult to force them to
return. Many were quickly aided and absorbed by members
of the existing Cuban community.

But the new refugees differed from those who had come
earlier. They were less educated, with fewer job skills; 12 per-

cent were black. Many were young adults who had grown up under a communist system, and they seemed less able to adapt to a free-enterprise economy, more reliant on government action and less on individual initiative. Their reasons for coming seemed primarily economic, although many also said they sought liberty or a new life. Cuba was experiencing a deteriorating economic situation brought on by crop failures.

The Cuban experience illustrates many of the trends in recent U. S. immigration history. The first-wave Cubans were warmly welcomed as the kind of immigrants the United States most likes to receive—enterprising, freedom-loving exiles from communism. The second-wave immigrants were less welcome. They came during a recession, and they were seen as economic exiles who would compete for jobs with other ethnic minorities here, particularly poor blacks. The United States was under pressure to take refugees from other countries, too—from Vietnam, Cambodia, and Haiti.

The Cubans here seem determined and able to thrive in American society, but not without feeling some nostalgia for what they have lost. Martinez became a U. S. citizen in 1967 and doubts he would ever go back because "my two sons were born here." But despite his adjustment to American life, he says, "I consider myself Cuban in the bottom of my heart; I was born there."

PUERTO RICANS

Puerto Ricans are not immigrants; they are born U. S. citizens and can move back and forth freely because of the commonwealth status of Puerto Rico. Their migration to the mainland, however, is an important part of the growing Hispanic impact on the United States. The Puerto Rican impact is characterized by a constant flow of people between the two

countries, a clash in cultures, a
vancement.

More than 3 million Puerto
and another 1.7 million live in t
Most Puerto Ricans have come t
during their lives. Each year thou
1972, however, 40,000 more ha
have left. So many have retur
style—maintained by "New Y
Juan. The movement back and
across the Mexican border. But f
is easier; they have no hassles
threats of deportation.

They migrate for the usual
ficient employment, and the lu
relatives. Despite its financial p
has unskilled and skilled jobs
reasonably cheap.

One of the reasons for retu
in general, Puerto Ricans have
States, certainly not as much as
dian family income for Puerto I
among Hispanics. Puerto Rican
ployment rate among Hispanics
are self-supporting, about 30 pe
in New York City receive son
country as a whole, 32 percent
below the poverty level.

In New York City, Puerto F
abuse, lead poisoning, cirrhosis
homicide-related deaths. Homi
gle cause of death there for P
tween the ages of fifteen and fo

second,
is third.

Pu
United
tively.
Mauric
the Bro
New Y
third H
strated
program
has evc
Ricans
centrati
more in

The
partly d
and a s
identify
and oth
spread t

Pu
land. B
turies in
there th
themsel
by race
America
panic in

DOMINI

Do
bean H

Republic shares with Haiti. Racially they have more in common with Caribbean blacks, but culturally—in language, colonial heritage, and Catholic religion—they are Hispanic.

Dominicans are the third largest immigrant group from Latin America, after Mexicans and Cubans. More than five hundred Dominicans apply to the U. S. consulate in the capital city of Santo Domingo each day for tourist or immigrant visas. When they are rejected, as 40 percent are, many come illegally instead. By the end of 1978, at least 300,000 Dominicans legally resided in the United States. If illegal immigrants are included, an estimated 500,000 Dominicans live in the New York metropolitan region, a number equivalent to 10 percent of the Dominican Republic population. Immigration seems to have declined somewhat in the 1970s, however, and return migration increased.

The stereotype of the Dominican migrant is of a member of the lower classes or a peasant, but studies show that most immigrants actually come from the middle classes and from the cities. A large majority are literate and better educated than the rest of their countrymen, and they emigrate in the prime of their productive lives, before age forty. Some of them may have lived in the cities only a short time before emigrating, however, and they may still have many rural ways.

They come to the United States in search of jobs, from a country with a 30 percent unemployment rate. Even unskilled, illegal workers can earn more in New York in a week than they could in Santo Domingo in a month. Though the country is stable and democratic, living standards are not high. In fact, one of the most lucrative businesses is providing American visas or work permits. "After the sugar industry, hustling visas has become the biggest business there is in the D. R.," commented a lawyer.

"People are so desperate to go they make large payments for nothing," the U. S. consul general said. Recently twenty-two Dominicans, each of whom had paid $1,500 to $3,000 for passage to Miami, died of asphyxiation in the ballast tank of a freighter as it was searched by officials. Many risk a trip in a small boat to Puerto Rico where they may be able to pass as Puerto Ricans and fly to New York.

They come illegally because of the long wait for visas, the lack of a preference system before 1977 to allocate positions, and the high visa-rejection rate. Most applicants are rejected because they have little money and few job skills and because their relatives already in the United States cannot prove they will be able to support them.

Dominicans tend to see immigration as a temporary way to help their families. In the *New York Times* survey, five out of six said they considered Santo Domingo, rather than New York City, their home. Of those who left before 1974, some 39 percent actually returned. They remain financially committed to the homeland, too, and to family members at home, sending back up to $12 million a year. A small village in Santo Domingo may be almost totally dependent on money sent from the United States. One family described New York as "the best place to get ahead, to improve your life, to live better," but the Dominican Republic as "the best place to be if you are down and out or have problems."

Socioeconomic class influences the decision of a Dominican to leave and determines whether he or she is likely to return. Members of the lower classes are more likely to leave because of unemployment; upper-class Dominicans often leave to attend American schools. Almost all members of the upper class eventually return; only about half of the middle class, one-quarter of the lower urban class, and one-tenth of the rural migrants go back. When those from the middle and upper classes return, they have often made and saved enough money to buy property.

Because they are dark-skinned, Dominicans experience more racial discrimination than other Hispanics in the United States. Even being identified on the basis of race rather than nationality is a new experience for Dominicans. Some try to pass as Puerto Ricans, to mask their illegal status or because Puerto Ricans have a slightly higher status. Nevertheless, second-generation Dominicans—those born here—have experienced some success. According to marriage records, 20.5 percent of Dominican bridegrooms in New York hold professional or managerial jobs.

For 90 percent of Dominican migrants, emigration means coming to New York. The money for the trip often comes as a gift or loan from relatives and friends already in the city. More than half settle on the Upper West Side of Manhattan in Washington Heights. They often form recreational associations, particularly soccer teams and leagues, but family ties remain the most important help in adapting to city life. Thus, Dominicans' patterns of family unity, contact with the homeland, and economic motivation are similar to those of other Hispanics and Caribbean peoples.

Central and South Americans

Except from contiguous Canada and Mexico, immigration from the Western Hemisphere has been only a trickle for many years. The United States is too far away from other Hispanic nations—geographically and psychologically—and the majority of Latin Americans are too poor even to consider moving. In 1976 only 22,706 immigrated from South America and 9,967 from Central America. But the picture has begun to change. Both legal and illegal immigration from Central and

South America is increasing. Border patrol agents along the Mexican border have noticed more OTMs—other than Mexicans—attempting to cross, having first made their way to Mexico from El Salvador, Guatemala, or another Latin nation.

The main push is from population growth. Birthrates have remained very high in Latin America while death rates—especially from communicable and infant-related diseases—have declined drastically. At its present annual growth rate of 2.7 percent, the population of Latin America will double in twenty-six years. The growth is particularly obvious in the capital cities of Central America. The population of Guatemala City increased from half a million in 1960 to 1.2 million in 1976. San Salvador, Tegucigalpa, Managua, San José, and Panama City also more than doubled.

These countries have been developing economically, producing more middle-class, skilled, and professional people. But the number of workers—even skilled—far exceeds the number of jobs available. Land is scarce, as it is divided and subdivided among sons or remains in the hands of large companies. Peasants pushed off the land or no longer able to eke out a living migrate to the cities. The new wealth from export crops and tourism seems to help only the elite.

Thus both the lower and middle classes have reasons, and some the wherewithal, to leave. Political instability, leading to violence, often provides the impetus. Recent political upheavals in the "troubled triangle" of Nicaragua, Guatemala, and El Salvador especially have prompted emigration.

Nicaragua came to American attention in July 1979 when Sandinist guerrillas overthrew the dictatorship of General Anastasio Somoza. Civilians fled the bloody civil war, and an estimated 10,000 came to Miami. In addition to the Miami community, an estimated 50,000 Nicaraguans live in the San Francisco Bay area, and 40,000 have settled in Los Angeles.

El Salvador is the poorest and most densely populated Latin American country, and recent political turbulence has convinced many Salvadoreans to leave. Many who cross the Mexican border say they are coming for political reasons— "because things are so bad in El Salvador." After thirteen Salvadoreans died in the Arizona desert in an attempt to enter this country, a *New York Times* article reported that "thousands of jobless Salvadoreans are trekking across Mexico in hope of finding work in the United States."

Elsewhere in Latin America, the need to emigrate is not so desperate, but the myth of the streets of gold still lures the hopeful. A garment worker who can make two or three dollars a day in Guatemala will make ten to fifteen dollars in the United States. Yet the tales of riches do not always ring true. "Their idea is you can come here, you become rich—everybody in this country is a millionaire," said one Guatemalan immigrant. "As far as my family is concerned, I am very rich. I have this nice home. But they don't know that you have to work harder than they have to work to make a living here."

Among South American immigrants, Colombians and Ecuadoreans are the most numerous. They settle mainly in New York, which has an estimated 300,000 Colombians and 150,000 to 200,000 Ecuadoreans.

Colombians began immigrating in the early 1960s following a decade of political violence. At first the middle class came—the highly trained professionals and technical personnel. In the late 1960s, more nonprofessional members of the middle class and the lower classes began coming. After 1970 the number of Colombian immigrants actually declined by almost half from about 11,000 in 1965 to approximately 6,000 in 1976.

While here, Colombians maintain close ties to their

homeland, even voting in Colombia's elections. About 3,000 voted at the consulate in 1970, and in 1974 a major candidate in the Colombian election campaigned in the Queens section of New York City. Many visit Colombia every two or three years, and most plan to return eventually. In response to a *New York Times* survey, 50 percent of Colombians said they considered New York City home and 50 percent said Colombia was home. They sent an estimated $250 million back home from Venezuela, Bolivia, and the United States during one eighteen-month period. Some save to buy property when they return.

Ecuadoreans are more settled, picking New York as home by a margin of three to two. The Ecuadorean community in Queens, New York City, is now well established. It has seventy Ecuadorean organizations, most devoted to soccer. The teams compete in the annual celebration of Ecuador's National Day in Flushing Meadow Park.

Nonetheless, Ecuadoreans also remain in close contact with those at home. And, like the Colombian candidate, the new president of Ecuador visited the New York City Ecuadorean community as a candidate in 1978.

Emigration from Central and South America fluctuates, then, with economic downswings and political upheavals. Many Latin emigrants go to other countries—Venezuela, Spain, Mexico, and Italy. But their immigration to this country is aided by the establishment of national communities here. As of March 1979, the United States had 2.2 million residents from Central and South America.

HISPANIC IMMIGRANTS are a growing and diverse group with a significant recent impact on U. S. cities. They have changed the tone of New York, Miami, and Los Angeles, where some see the old confrontation between the European powers in the

New World being replayed. The cultural descendants of the French, Dutch, and English who dominated in North America and the Spanish and Portuguese who took over the rest of the hemisphere are facing off again.

Hispanics see the contrast as between hot and cold: the warm-hearted, spontaneous, emotional Latin versus the cool, efficient, rational Anglo-Saxon. And values, as well as personalities, conflict. Hispanics do not like what they see happening to American families: the high divorce rate, the subordination of family to career, and the trend toward smaller, nuclear families without the nearness and support of aunts, uncles, grandparents, and cousins. Their views of education and child-rearing also differ. Hispanics see education as a means of acquiring good behavior, discipline, and morals rather than knowledge. In child-rearing, respect for adults is most important. American racial attitudes also alienate Hispanics; racial mixing is much more acceptable to them.

Some Hispanics say the cultural differences are so strong that Hispanics will not "melt" in the mythical melting pot, that they will succeed in maintaining a separate language and culture to a much greater extent than previous immigrants. A Cuban family in their new suburban Miami home assured the interviewer that because of their pride in their heritage, Cubans would not assimilate. "We're very stubborn; I don't believe we'll ever melt." They described themselves as having too much fun to change and used the analogy of black beans and rice: it's nice to serve them together, but they shouldn't be mixed.

American reaction to Hispanic immigrants has varied, often according to the state of the economy. Hispanics are aware of resentment. "They see us as stupid and violent people," one Hispanic New Yorker said. They "see us as rowdy" in "the manifestation of our happiness in dance and song," said another. According to a recent study in New York, an Hispanic convicted of a drug offense is more likely to be sent to prison, more likely to receive a harsher sentence, and less likely to be placed on probation than a non-Hispanic.

Hispanics have only begun to be more assertive in American society. Economic survival was their first goal. According to the 1970 census, Spanish-origin Americans earned about 70 percent as much as average Americans. Their unemployment rate was almost twice that of the rest of the population. Only 25 percent of the men worked in white-collar jobs, compared with 41 percent of men of all origins. They were also more likely to live in substandard housing, to receive inferior schooling, to be affected by crime, alcohol, and drug abuse, and to be without health insurance or pensions.

Politics has begun to offer a way to attack these problems. Hispanics have an organizational advantage over previous immigrant groups in that they speak the same language. Other differences have kept them apart, however: economic status, degree of attachment to the United States, and pride in nationality.

Different groups are potentially strong in different parts of the country. Cubans have begun to affect Florida politics, particularly in Tampa and Miami. Puerto Ricans, though numerically strong, have not been politically successful in New York. But in the Southwest, Mexican-Americans have been able to swing elections. Twice as many Hispanic-Americans—800,000—were registered to vote in Texas in 1980 as in 1976. The emergence of a second or third generation of Mexican-Americans with middle-class goals—home ownership, college and professional educations for their children, and recognition in society—provides a political base.

Hispanics are addressing the area of education, often demanding bilingual classes. In Los Angeles city schools 40 percent of the pupils are Hispanic, and their enrollment is economically vital to the school system. Hispanic enrollment in New York City's senior colleges (City University of New York) has leaped 500 percent in the last decade.

Hispanics are far from speaking with a united voice, however. Colombians don't yet want to become involved in U. S. politics. Puerto Ricans are torn between working within the U. S. political process and seeking Puerto Rican independence. Mexicans resent what they see as the government's favoritism toward Cubans.

Hispanic immigration seems likely to continue to increase and with it the involvement of Hispanics in U. S. society. The probability is that each culture will give a bit, and the United States will inevitably become more Latin.

Chapter III
THE NEW ASIANS

If the lamp pole had feet, it would come here.

New Asian immigrants to the United States are making up for lost time. For decades, they were specifically excluded from the welcome to immigrants. In 1917 U. S. immigration law put Asian countries into an "Asiatic Barred Zone," whose nationals were barred from immigrating. Until 1952 they were not given even token quotas, and Asians were not allowed to become citizens.

All that is beginning to seem like ancient history. Since 1965 Asians have been on an equal footing with every other nationality, and Asian immigration has increased 625 percent. It now numbers about 150,000 annually, outnumbering European and matching Western Hemisphere immigration. About 38,000 Filipinos come each year, 31,000 Koreans, 25,000 Chinese (including those from the People's Republic, Taiwan, and Hong Kong), and 18,000 Indians. Thailand, Vietnam, Japan, Pakistan, and Iran also send several thousand.

Many Asian countries have developed waiting lists for those who want immigrant visas, even sons and daughters of U. S. citizens. The backlog has affected the kind of people who come. A person from the Philippines, for example, almost has to be a nurse or a doctor in order to emigrate. Of all Asians admitted in 1975–1976, some 64 percent came as relatives of citizens or aliens; 20 percent came under occupational preference.

Orientals were excluded so long because Americans feared their potentially large numbers, competition for jobs, and the vast difference in cultures. Hispanics may speak a different language, but Spanish shares with English common roots in the Latin language. Hispanics may be predominantly Catholic, but Catholicism is no longer a foreign religion, but a familiar part of the American scene. Asians speak many languages vastly different from the Romance languages and practice less familiar religions (except for Christian Koreans). And, if Hispanics are perceived as warm and exuberant, Asians seem cool and quiet.

The Asian imprint has been strongest on the West Coast and in New York City. Los Angeles has the world's largest concentration of Koreans outside the Orient and also the largest concentration of Samoans outside Samoa. New York City had an Oriental population of at most 60,000 in 1965; now it has an estimated 200,000 new Asians, and some say 400,000. Twenty years ago, most Orientals in New York City were Chinese who lived in Chinatown. Now there are Koreans, Vietnamese, Cambodians, Laotians, Thais, Filipinos, and Japanese.

The official U. S. reaction to Asians has varied with the nation's foreign policy. During World War II, Japanese-Americans were suspected of disloyalty and gathered into internment camps. Now, as allies and trade partners, the Japanese are welcomed. Koreans are received on a similar basis. Southeast Asian refugees were welcomed in the late 1970s because they were exiles from a situation created partly by U. S. foreign policy.

Whereas Asians' letters home in the first half of the twentieth century reported hostility and repression, letters—and the money in them—sent home in the last ten years have been more encouraging. Thus, new immigrants have been pulled by the possibility of economic gain and a positive image of America and pushed by conditions in their own countries: limited opportunities for advancement, poverty, authoritarian political regimes, or chaotic civil war.

"Sometimes I can see that you do not know you are so lucky," comments Cac Thanh Lee, a Vietnamese urologist. "We have a four-room apartment here, much better than the studio in Saigon. We are not free in Vietnam, in our action, in our thinking. We have a saying, 'If the lamp pole had feet, it would come here.' "

Once here, Asians find language a great barrier because English, with its tongue-twisting consonants, is vastly different from their native speech. They tend to remain within their own communities until they are able to overcome the language problem. But the new Asians do not remain in the old ghettos—the Chinatowns of San Francisco and New York. They have moved out to the boroughs and suburbs.

The new Asians have been far more successful than their predecessors, mainly because the United States welcome has been much warmer. The stereotypical Asian of years ago was someone who worked in a restaurant, laundry, or garment factory—businesses they resorted to when forced out of jobs Americans wanted. But the new Asians have diversified. The Filipino nurse, the Indian engineer, the Korean pharmacist or fruit and vegetable store proprietor, and the Vietnamese fisherman are the new identities. Though materially satisfied, however, Asians have found the cultural adjustment difficult, as a closer look at the predominant groups will show.

Filipinos and the Brain Drain

Many of the new Asian immigrants are part of the brain drain mentioned earlier—the emigration of educated and skilled people from developing countries to countries that offer more opportunity. Indian doctors come here for further training and decide to stay here to continue research they could not do at home. Korean engineers emigrate when they cannot find engineering jobs in South Korea. Filipino nurses can earn higher salaries here.

This migration of trained professionals and technicians began in the 1960s. Before then, immigrants were more likely to be unskilled or poor. In the period from 1907 to 1923 only 2.6 percent of immigrants were professional and technical workers; from 1973 to 1976, the percentage was 25.5. One journalist has paraphrased the inscription on the Statue of Liberty to read, "Give me your gifted, your educated few, yearning to strike it rich."

To strike it rich is not the only reason for coming, however, and the receiving country usually gains as much as the immigrant does. In the mid-1970s, for example, one of every five doctors in this country was a graduate of a foreign medical school. The influx of foreign doctors occurred because the United States was not training enough doctors at home. It was less expensive to import doctors whose medical education was already paid for. The sending countries, such as India, the Philippines, Pakistan, and Korea, were educating large numbers of nurses and doctors who did not remain to serve their own populations. The same was true in other scientific fields.

The Republic of the Philippines is an example of the brain drain in action. Erlinda Nool is in many ways typical of the immigrant professional. She came from a small town in the province of Pangasinan, where the Ilocano dialect is spoken. Family ties are strong in these "barrios," and maintaining congenial relations with fellow workers, village friends, and relatives is important. Education—six years of elementary and four years of high school—is valued and equally available to men and women.

Before World War II, most of the Filipinos who immigrated to the United States were either students or laborers who came to work on the plantations in Hawaii or to take jobs in the Pacific Coast states. Others were sailors on the East Coast. Many came without wives and family, which resulted in settlements of single men. Erlinda Nool's grandfather went to Hawaii to work when her mother was seven. He never returned, but he sent money home.

After World War II about 1,000 Filipinos came here each year, still to the West Coast and Hawaii. In the early 1960s about 3,000 came each year. Then the number began to increase rapidly. From 1965 to 1974 Filipino immigration increased 950 percent. By 1976 some 37,000 came in one year—more than any other nationality except Mexican.

Not only did the numbers increase but the occupations of the immigrants also changed. By the mid-1960s doctors, nurses, pharmacists, dentists, engineers, teachers, and accountants were coming—the brain drain. Five hundred Filipino physicians and surgeons worked in Chicago alone. More than 14 percent of the nurses employed by New York City hospitals are from the Philippines, where many have been recruited by the city. By the mid-1970s there were more Filipino doctors than American black doctors in the United States.

Why were they leaving the barrios to fill hospital staff shortages in American cities? Some reasons are the large number of educated young people, the lack of suitable jobs, and the lower salaries and status given professionals in the Philippines. A household survey in the early 1960s in the Philippines located 35,000 college graduates without jobs. Filipino students surveyed in the United States said they thought they could accomplish more abroad in their professions and that the status of professionals is higher abroad.

Erlinda Nool spoke of the severe overcrowding and high cost of living in Manila. Housing is expensive there. A room shared with several other people in a private house or apartment is considered cheap at 350 pesos per person per month. (Seven and a half pesos are equal to one U. S. dollar.) A registered nurse in the Philippines earns only about 500 to 600 pesos a month. Items like an ice cream cone or a single apple cost more than a dollar. The attraction of a starting salary of $15,000 in the United States is obvious.

One characteristic of Filipino immigration, and of Indian immigration as well, is the high number of educated women who come. In New York City in 1970 the ratio of Filipino women to men was 113 to 100, and the women earned a median income of $6,022 (well above the $2,328 median for all U. S. women).

Adjustment to American life is easier for the professionals. Many have jobs lined up before they arrive. But some face licensing exams. One physician who came here with sixteen years' experience in medicine worked first as a janitor and then as a meat cutter. "They thought I was very good at separating the meat from the bone," he said. Some professionals have trouble proving their credentials or find their college degrees equated with finishing only two years of college here. To screen out nurses who may not meet state requirements, the United States now requires them to pass a pre-board exam in the Philippines before they may come under the occupational preference category. Many circumvent this by coming under the relative-preference category instead.

Not all Filipino immigrants are professionals, of course. Many more are coming now as relatives of those already here. Those Filipinos not in professions, white-collar jobs, or household jobs are concentrated in agricultural work and in the navy as mess stewards. In 1970 there were more Filipino volunteers working as valets, cooks, cabin boys, and dishwashers in the U. S. Navy than there were sailors in the entire navy of the Philippines. In Hawaii Filipinos constitute 50 percent of the membership of the International Ladies' Garment Workers' Union (ILGWU), 40 percent of the AFL-CIO hotel and restaurant workers' union, and 25 percent of the Teamsters' union.

Unlike the Koreans and Chinese, Filipinos do not often start their own businesses. One Filipino leader in Hawaii said, "We are not sophisticated, businesswise, like the Chinese. Economically we are at the bottom level. The only way we are going to make it is through education and [entrance into the] professions, and with that, [we will] gain respect in the total community." Filipinos place a high value on education, and their children do not have a high drop-out rate.

Although about two-thirds of Filipino immigrants have at least a high school education, they, too, experience the problems of mastering English, finding jobs that match their skills, or finding any jobs at all. Some end up on welfare. The elderly, especially, are poor. In New York City, 3.1 percent of Filipinos receive public assistance, and 24 percent of the Filipino elderly are poor.

Filipinos are concentrated, like many immigrant groups,

on the coasts and in large midland cities like Chicago. According to the 1970 census, 73 percent were living in the West, in California and Hawaii. More than 10,000 Filipinos lived in New York State, Illinois, and Washington. Those who come to New York are more affluent. They tend to move on to the suburbs or other parts of the country. Experts estimate that the U. S. Filipino population in 1980 was about 650,000.

As a group, Filipinos have not been highly visible to most Americans, except in hospitals. Like Hispanics they have encountered racial discrimination, although professionals experience it less than the earlier laborers did. Their hospital jobs place them in competition with members of other ethnic minorities, particularly blacks. Patients, too, can be race conscious. Erlinda Nool described how some white patients will ask to talk to another nurse. "If it's a choice between a white nurse and me, they'll ask for the white nurse. If it's between me and a black, they'll ask for me. That's the way it goes: white, Filipino, black."

Ms. Nool plans to return to the Philippines to retire because, she says, "I don't want to become old and go into a nursing home here." She spoke of the contrast between life here and there. "You have material things, here, but life is not easy. We don't work over there like we do here. There's not too much pressure. But you do earn more money here. My sisters think the United States is really a rosy place, but I tell them, 'Prepare yourselves—no maids here.' [In the Philippines middle-class families can usually afford maids.] Here you do everything yourself—the shopping, the laundry." She noted that men do more of the household work here, even the laundry. Here families are not as close-knit, with fewer relatives living together.

Despite their parents' desire to return, the Nool children

are well on their way to becoming thoroughly American. After two weeks in kindergarten, Jennifer reported, "Mommy you don't speak good English." When Ms. Nool explained that was because she wasn't born here, Jennifer replied, "But I am an American; I speak good English."

Koreans

After Mexico and the Philippines, South Korea sent more immigrants to the United States in the late 1970s than any other single country. This is surprising, given the relatively small population of the country—37 million as compared with Mexico's 67 million, the Philippines' 46 million, or India's 638 million. Nor has the Korean immigration been that noticeable. Koreans have clustered in urban areas such as Los Angeles, New York, and Honolulu and mingled with other immigrant groups.

Like the Filipinos, Koreans came in earlier decades but then were severely restricted. In 1902 the Korean government encouraged emigration by opening an office where Hawaiian sugar plantation owners could recruit laborers. More than 7,000 Koreans—mostly unemployed men from seaport towns—came in two years. But by mid-1905, the Korean government had cut off emigration to protect its nationals from exploitation. Small Korean communities remained in Los Angeles, San Francisco, Honolulu, Seattle, Chicago, and New York. The immigrants who came then founded Christian churches where they settled.

In 1917 Koreans were excluded as part of the Asiatic barred zone and ruled ineligible for citizenship. Then Korean immigration resumed gradually after World War II under the quota of 100 set in 1952. Many came, too, as members of the immediate families of U. S. citizens: the wives, children, or adopted children of U. S. servicemen who had been in Korea during the Korean War. Others came to escape the internal upheavals of the war.

Immigration to the United States increased rapidly after the change in U. S. immigration law and after Park Chung Hee became a dictatorial president in Korea. By 1974 it had increased more than 1,000 percent since 1965, and Korea had reached the status of third largest sending country. About 31,000 Koreans came here in 1976. The new Koreans settled predominantly on the West Coast in California, Hawaii, and Washington, in the New York metropolitan area, and in Illinois and Pennsylvania.

Who are the new Koreans? They have come predominantly from the upper and middle classes and are well educated. They did not emigrate because of unemployment, poverty, or even primarily for political reasons but because there is a surplus of college-educated men and women in Korea. "South Koreans make up the best-educated group of immigrants ever to come to this country in large numbers," said an American professor. "And they are coming here because they are so highly educated. No country its size needs as many college graduates as South Korea has."

"This is a country of more and more: opportunities, knowledge, wealth," said Hyun Chul Kim, a civil engineer who is working in New York as a salesman.

Most Koreans leave urban areas in Korea and settle in urban areas here where friends and relatives are already well established. A network of professional and social associations helps with jobs and personal support.

Even for professionals, however, finding a job is not easy. Like the Filipinos, many face licensing barriers. Each state regulates who may become a dentist, pharmacist, teacher, or architect, and most require applicants to pass an exam. Applicants with foreign training may need additional study to improve their command of English. Many states will not license professionals either until they become citizens. Some professionals take whatever jobs they can find, hoping eventually to work in a position that uses their skills and training.

Koreans who are not professionals have proved very resourceful. They have become noted for opening small businesses. The Korean fruit and vegetable store has become an urban landmark in some areas. Such stores require little capital—the cost of the rent, adding machine, refrigeration equipment, and produce—and can use the labor power of a family. They do not require extensive knowledge of English, but at the same time they allow the owners to develop the most necessary language skills. Restaurants and wholesale concerns dealing in electronic equipment and textiles also are common.

Not all have adjusted well. In 1973 about 20 percent of the Koreans in Los Angeles were unemployed, even though most were well educated. Three thousand were receiving welfare. Women who must work have an especially difficult adjustment. They come from a patriarchal society where women have traditionally been barred from intellectual training. Unlike Filipino and Indian women who come here, Korean women are not prepared for careers. In fact, 24 percent of Korean women who work in New York City earn less than $4,000 a year. When the woman does find a job, tensions often arise at home.

Many of the more recent arrivals from Korea have just a high school education and must look for manual work. "We came for a better life," a garment worker said, "but we have not found it better yet. It is work, work, work." Also, 40 percent arrive speaking no English; only 10 percent speak it fluently.

As a group Koreans who have immigrated have done very well. Most start with the advantage of education. According to the 1970 census, 81 percent were high school graduates and 53 percent were also college graduates. The median salary of Korean-American men was close to that of the total population. Members of less highly educated groups have been arriving, however, and the success figures may be more varied in the 1980 census.

Like other immigrant groups, the Koreans also experience strain between the generations—the immigrant parents and their children. The youth have developed a different culture from the adults. The young people become friends with members of different ethnic groups, and the girls demand equal rights. They reject even the common food of the Korean home, kim chee, because it leaves their breath smelling of garlic and spices. Their search for freedom and their accommodation to the host society seem like disrespect to the parents and a threat to the family.

Even with education and material success, the immigrant may not be happy. One adolescent who came in 1973 with his father describes the gap between his own expectations (and those of his countrymen) and the reality here: "If I come to America, I thought that America was really heaven country. I saw so many movie. I saw cars; everyone drives car. If I go to America, I can drive. I can watch TV, everything. I thought I was really heading to heaven. But that's wrong. You have to try to make heaven. . . . Before they come here [everybody] think of this country as heaven."

Chinese

The Chinese are perhaps the best known Asian immigrants to the United States, but they are no longer the most numerous. The number of immigrants from the People's Republic of China, Taiwan, and Hong Kong, and including even ethnic Chinese from Southeast Asia, has been exceeded by the number of Filipinos and Koreans, despite the smaller populations of their countries. About 24,000 Chinese have come here each year in recent years.

The Chinese have had a unique status as immigrants. When they first came to work on the railroads and in mining, their right to immigrate was unrestricted. After the railroads were built and the discovery of gold exacerbated tensions between native and foreign workers, they were largely forbidden to come here. The only way they could enter was as businessmen (and many "businessmen" were made overnight) or as close relatives of immigrants already here. The latter possibility gave rise to "paper sons" and the "slot system." A Chinese immigrant would go back to China for a long visit. When he returned to the United States, he would claim that a son or daughter had been born to him and secure the documents to prove it. Later he could sell this slot for a "paper son" to a fellow Chinese who wanted to immigrate.

After World War I, a quota of 105 immigrants a year was set for China, and few came until the 1950s when a wave of refugees flooded Hong Kong as the communists took over China. About 15,000 refugees, most of whom had waited years for visas, were allowed to enter the United States from 1962 to 1965. Thus, the Chinese living here before 1965 were the much older immigrants and their descendants, a few families, and the refugees of the 1950s. They were concentrated in California, New York, and Hawaii.

When Asians were admitted equally after 1968, Chinese immigration boomed. The population of New York City's Chinatown increased from 4,000 in 1960 to 24,000 in 1970. The total Chinese population of the New York City area had grown to 130,000 or 140,000 by 1980 and had spread from Chinatown to the Upper West Side, Queens, the Flatbush area of Brooklyn, and Great Neck, Long Island. California and Hawaii, too, had larger Chinese populations, but much of their growth came from an increase in the birthrate rather than from immigration. The Chinese have preferred living in U. S. cities since the nineteenth century when Americans in urban areas were more tolerant.

Chinese immigration has been facilitated by the now friendly relations between the United States and China. American citizens of Chinese ancestry submitted more than five thousand petitions to the new U. S. embassy in Peking in its first year, asking that immediate kin be allowed to immigrate. And an American consulate opened in September 1979 in Canton; there are at least a thousand American-born Chinese in surrounding Guangdong province who are eligible to return here.

Who are the new Chinese? They are young, averaging between twenty and twenty-nine, with women outnumbering men. They are largely peasants or members of the working class, unlike many of the better-educated Japanese, Koreans, and Filipinos. Many have no more than a high school education and do not speak English.

They come mainly from the district of Toishan and the areas near the city of Canton and the mouth of the Pearl River. Because it is difficult to obtain an exit visa from the Chinese government, many flee to Hong Kong first and embark from there. (Canton is near Hong Kong.) Chinese immigrants also come to the United States from Taiwan, Southeast Asia, Trinidad, Jamaica, and Cuba. Whole families tend to arrive together, instead of sending a young male first to establish himself.

They come to join relatives, and they come for traditional economic reasons. Free public education is a particular attraction. Education in Hong Kong is unaffordable for most; tuition is required even for elementary school, and college is very expensive.

"Now, when I was young, my mother wouldn't let me go to school," one immigrant said. "I had to work because I was the oldest son. So one thing I resolved was to let my children have an education. That's why I decided to come here, for my children."

Another reason for leaving is overpopulation. In Hong Kong some people rent bed space on eight-hour shifts. "When your time is up, they wake you so the next person can have the bed."

Once here, working-class newcomers often find their first job in the Chinese community where knowing English is not necessary. The Chinatowns of New York, San Francisco, and Los Angeles provide a buffer for the uneducated and unskilled, and they offer jobs in three traditional areas: laundries, restaurants, and the garment industry.

Recently, these areas of employment have been hard pressed. The small Chinese laundry, for example, is being replaced by large-scale steam laundries, laundromats, home washers and dryers, and permanent-press fabrics. The number of Chinese laundries in New York had declined from 3,000 to 1,000 by the mid-1970s. Many of those remaining send the laundry out and serve only as collection and distribution services.

The costs of running a restaurant have risen, too, and the industry has reached its saturation point. Only approximately

120 of the highest-paid positions as cooks remain in New York City's Chinatown. The majority of Chinese are in low-paying busboy or kitchen-helper jobs. Even though the number of such jobs has diminished, 36 percent of the Chinese men in New York City remain service workers, largely in restaurants.

Women take jobs in garment factories in Chinatown where they can remain close to home and work irregular hours. About 44 percent of the Chinese working women in New York are employed as operators, mainly of sewing machines. The ILGWU in New York has more than 5,000 Asian members (mostly Chinese) out of a total membership of 19,000.

As these jobs diminish, new arrivals find work as janitors, deliverymen, gas station attendants, grocery and market workers, and pastry, or dim sum, chefs in Chinese tea houses. For such immigrants, the hours are long and the pay is low. In the early 1970s men earned from $3,500 to $7,000 a year and women from $1,500 to $3,600. Out of these low wages many families hope to save enough in a few years to open their own restaurants or businesses.

In addition to the working-class immigrants, the new Chinese include a high proportion of professionals and technicians who are eventually able to find jobs that match their training.

Some upper-class immigrants have received training and earned advanced degrees at American universities and have become highly respected scientists, architects, scholars, and financiers here. By 1970, some 21.2 percent of American Chinese were in the professions. The majority—59 percent—still worked in personal services, in manufacturing, and in the wholesale and retail trade.

The rising number of Chinese professionals in the

United States has been attributed to decreasing discrimination, an increasing number of native-born Chinese-Americans, the 1949 communist takeover when many Chinese students in the United States decided to remain, and the easing of immigration restrictions. The Chinese are concentrated in a few professions: 25 percent in engineering, for instance, and 11.6 percent in college teaching. The three subjects taught by most of the college teachers are engineering, physics, and mathematics. This concentration outside the more verbal humanities has been attributed in part to the initial language barrier.

The new immigrants—called FOBs by other Chinese-Americans for "fresh off the boat"—are a contrast to the older group of immigrants. Those from Hong Kong, especially, are cosmopolitan and urbanized; they know their way around a city. They come here with their families, intending to stay. The old-timers seem to live more in the past, tied to a China that no longer exists. Between the two are the second-generation Chinese-Americans who have discarded many of the old ways and, through the educational system, begun to move into the mainstream of American culture.

The newcomers' ability to adjust is related to their social class. The professionals buy homes in the suburbs and have little tie to the Chinatowns, except perhaps to go there for an occasional meal. The working-class immigrants have a much more difficult time and must depend on the Chinatown resources, however meager, for jobs, housing, and neighbors who speak the same language. They arrived in the Chinatowns of New York, San Francisco, and Los Angeles at a time when the neighborhoods were deteriorating. The influx of new immigrants reinvigorated the Chinatowns but also put them under severe strain. With the second highest population density rate in the country, San Francisco's Chinatown, for example, had a hard time finding room for anyone else. Already, 77 percent of its housing was substandard according to the city's codes. The one public housing project has a waiting list of at least four years. Unemployment was also high, with many underemployed. The area had the highest suicide rate in the nation in 1969, and there were only two Chinese-speaking psychiatrists in San Francisco. Almost 60 percent of the families in New York's Chinatown live below the federal poverty level.

Under these conditions, it is not surprising that conflict arose between the old-time residents and the "interlopers." Immigrant youth found themselves segregated by language, unable to succeed in school, and left to themselves while parents worked long hours. They began to challenge the traditional community authority. In the process, Chinatowns ceased to be the isolated ethnic enclaves they once were. According to the author of a study called *Longtime Californ,* "never again will a community of Chinese in America exist with the degree of isolation that characterized Chinatown in the past."

The second-generation Chinese have been responsible for some of the break from the past. They became more assertive during the minority-rights movements of the 1960s. Through education they entered new areas of employment. The new immigrants have helped break the ghetto pattern, too. They bring more ego strength with them because they have not experienced as much discrimination. "They are used to thinking that if they try hard enough they'll make it," said a social worker. They have not been as suppressed as some of the older Chinese-Americans, and "they still have the will to fight in order to improve."

Nonetheless the working-class immigrants' adjustment has not been easy. Instead of participating in a small family business, most work long hours away from home, leaving children to look after themselves. Although they place much of their hope for betterment in their children, the lack of supervision at home does not help the child who is having trouble adjusting in school. The close and stable family life that has characterized Chinatowns of the past is threatened by the new work pattern. An increase in juvenile delinquency has resulted.

A housewife who left China and came to Fresno, California, in 1960 found her main problems were being unable to speak English, having no warm clothes in a cold climate, and finding suitable housing. She is satisfied now that "we have a house to live in [an apartment in a low-income development], rice to eat." But she remembers her initial disappointment: "We always talked about coming to America, thinking that to come to America, to the Gold Hill, was great. Who would know when we arrived it would be like this?"

East Indians

Like the Filipinos and Koreans, the East Indians from India, Pakistan, and Bangladesh are brain-drain immigrants. They are the elite of their native countries. Of East Indians in New York City in the 1970s, about 90 percent held college degrees or professional diplomas. The average family income was above $15,000 a year. They were middle-class, urban, property-owning engineers, doctors, college teachers, accountants, and businessmen who seemed to integrate easily into American professional society. Men abandoned their native dress for the conventional business suit.

Immigration of East Indians, too, was restricted for many years, and Indians have come to the United States in large numbers only since the 1960s. In 1976, a total of 17,487 came here from India, an increase of almost 3,000 percent over 1965 when only 582 came. From Pakistan, there were

2,888 immigrants in 1976, as compared with 187 in 1965. As recently as 1970 there were only 13,000 East Indians in the entire country. Ten times that many have come since.

The pattern has been for a professional man to come with his wife and children. The immigrants are young; 60 percent are under thirty. About 50 percent of Indian immigrants and 25 percent of Pakistanis are from the professional classes.

East Indians in the Northeast are concentrated in New York, and in the north central United States, in Chicago. The 30,000 Indians in the New York metropolitan area live primarily in Queens, Long Island, Westchester County, and New Jersey. The region has twenty weekly Indian newspapers, twenty Indian travel agents, and ten Indian radio programs.

Although East Indians have moved fairly quickly into American life, they have a strong desire to maintain their own culture. Only about 10 to 15 percent have become citizens. Although they regard the United States as favorable to their professional development, they often prefer India for its culture and quality of life.

Religiosity is particularly strong. There are five Indian temples in Queens. East Indian religions have also made an impact on Americans, gaining converts to the Sikh religion, to Guru Majara Ji—leader of the Divine Light Mission—to yoga, and Hare Krishna. In 1974 an estimated 150,000 Americans were Sikhs, marked by their turbans.

The Indians have been compared to Jewish immigrants in their economic behavior. They emphasize saving money and buying property. Their leisure centers on family and friends. Because they are educated in the British tradition, they have no language problem. And they are well organized, already exerting strength as a pressure group. The Association of Indians in America was successful in obtaining a reclassification of Indians as Asian Indians instead of Caucasians in the 1980 census. This is a practical, political advantage because it makes Indians eligible for minority status and equal opportunity in employment.

Not all professional East Indians who immigrate intend to stay here permanently. But once here, they find high status both professionally and socially, good incomes, and favorable opportunities and resources for continuing work in their fields. Indians report a wide difference between working conditions at home and abroad. They find more intellectual companionship from colleagues abroad and a higher quality of assistants. There are also large numbers of job seekers in India.

An Indian doctor, for example, came here for further training in pediatrics. She described U. S. pediatrics as much more advanced than in India, with nurseries for newborn infants, intensive care facilities, and means to care for premature babies. Passing the Foreign Medical School Graduates (FMSG) exam in India, Dr. N (a pseudo-initial) applied for an internship in a New Jersey community hospital because her brother was living in that state. The hospital promised her the job and sent her an airplane ticket; she was to repay the hospital from her first six months' salary. (The Indian government restricts the amount of money that can be sent or taken out of the country.) She now serves an urban community in a family health clinic in Brooklyn.

Dr. N has not returned to India to live and work, primarily because she has married an Indian who wants to stay here. She lives in a suburban home with her husband, two children ages seven and four, and her mother-in-law. Her children speak English and prefer hot dogs and hamburgers to Indian food. Other members of her family have immigrated, too. Her oldest brother, an engineer, is a U. S. citizen.

Dr. N listed some of the reasons East Indians stay in the United States: the inducement of advanced training, career opportunities, marriage and family ties. A mid-1970s study of Indian students here revealed that 90 percent had financed their own education and felt no clear obligation to return to India. The author of the survey described the students as basically interested in careers and not particularly idealistic, patriotic, or self-sacrificing. An Indian electrical engineer here commented, "I don't believe that if I went to school there I am bound to work the rest of my life without doing any betterment to myself or without really doing what I want to do."

The Indian government has tried recently to keep professionals from leaving. It limits the amount of money that can be taken out of the country so that a would-be graduate student often must obtain a fellowship or assistantship from the American university he or she wants to attend. It also stopped giving the FMSG exam in the late 1960s. Students in India's medical schools must now sign a bond promising to work for five years in a rural area when they graduate or pay the government back for the cost of their training. Pakistan, too, has tried to limit emigration.

Southeast Asian Refugees

Tieng Huynh was working in navy security in South Vietnam when the North Vietnamese invaded Saigon in April 1975. Ordered to leave immediately and warned that "if we stay we die," he fled on a Vietnamese navy boat to the South China Sea, where he joined about 7,000 other refugees on a U. S. Navy ship. He left behind his wife, who was pregnant, and a son. He has heard from his family only twice since then.

Joining the U. S. Seventh Fleet, the refugees went to Guam. Huynh then went to Indian Town Gap, Pennsylvania, and stayed there until he and four other men moved to a small town in Iowa, sponsored by a Lutheran church.

Huynh's first job was picking apples. He held a factory job and then began working twelve to fourteen hours a day, seven days a week in construction, which eventually paid him more than $9 an hour. Huynh said the long hours were good because they helped him forget the life he had left. He has tried to get his family out, but the North Vietnamese claim no knowledge of them.

The Indo-Chinese are unique among Asian immigrants because they came here as refugees. They did not come voluntarily, seeking to better themselves; they came only after being forced out of their homelands for predominantly political reasons.

The first major wave began in the spring of 1975 when the North Vietnamese took over Saigon and the Americans evacuated. The first to leave were the rich, probably the only really voluntary immigrants. Also trying to leave were people who had worked for the U. S. government, the police, the army or navy, and those who had worked for American companies. Many were helped by the government or private firms. Even for them it was hard to get out. The last airline flights from Tansonnhut airport were jammed. Pictures of Vietnamese trying to cling to helicopters lifting off from the roof of the U. S. embassy appeared on the front pages of American newspapers.

In that first wave, more than 135,000 Vietnamese came to the United States. Such a large number from one country could be admitted only by the attorney general, using his parole power to admit refugees in an emergency. The refugees were urbanites of high occupational status; most spoke some

English and brought money with them; 85 percent had held white-collar jobs, and 48 percent had a secondary school education, which in Vietnam had led to middle-level government positions.

Although these first refugees hoped to return eventually, they adjusted fairly well. Congress authorized an Indo-Chinese refugee program that provided aid and funds for resettlement. By the end of 1975 all the spring evacuees had been resettled—the largest number of refugees ever resettled in this country in such a short period.

A smaller stream of Indo-Chinese immigrants, including Laotians and Cambodians, continued to arrive until 1979 when the "boat people" began appearing on the high seas, in overcrowded, leaky crafts, often short or completely out of food or water. They were mainly ethnic Chinese forced out of South Vietnam. The government had given them the choice of leaving or moving to a new economic zone to develop new land, probably through hard labor. Many of their businesses had been nationalized and confiscated, and most had to pay as much as $3,000 for the privilege of leaving. They were further preyed on by pirates at sea who robbed them and sometimes raped the women. Refugees who came by land to Thailand from Laos and especially Cambodia were fleeing starvation and civil war.

The boat people put to sea with no certain destination. While Americans reacted with sympathy from a distance, the countries on whose shores they landed soon felt overrun and unable to provide for them.

Between 1975 and October 1979 the United States had accepted 290,000 Indo-Chinese. The 95,000 who came in 1979 were 71 percent Vietnamese, 23 percent Laotian, and 6 percent Cambodian. The relatively sudden pressure to admit a large number of refugees had revealed inadequacies in

American immigration policy. Congress reexamined our refugee policy and subsequently passed a new Refugee Act in 1980 (see Chapter VIII).

The later arrivals were poorer, less skilled, less educated, and less literate even in their own languages than the 1975 group. They had one advantage, however, in that many of their countrymen had already established communities in the United States and paved the way.

The Indo-Chinese were resettled in the United States by means of a new process. The 1975 group spent a few months on Guam and Wake Island in the Pacific, then went on to processing centers in the United States to await sponsors. The sponsors, many of them religious groups or churches, were obligated to help the refugees find jobs and housing and settle into a new community. The federal government reimbursed local governments for cash and medical assistance provided to the refugees and gave the sponsor $250 for each refugee. (This amount was increased to $450 in 1979, but the Church World Service estimated that the actual cost was $1,000 to $3,000 for each refugee.) Language- and employment-training programs were also provided.

When the boat people came in 1979, the government followed a somewhat different process of resettlement. As refugee camps became overcrowded in the countries of first asylum, the Philippines agreed to host a United Nations–supported halfway camp and processing center. Potential U. S. immigrants were first interviewed and screened at the original camps. If accepted, they were moved to Bataan where they stayed until they could be moved directly to their new homes. Four in ten headed for California; one in ten went to Texas.

The state of Iowa provides an example of how resettlement actually worked. As the boat people began arriving in

Southeast Asian countries, Iowa let it be known that the refugees were welcome there. More than four thousand eventually went to Iowa, a larger number in proportion to its population than any other country or state except Australia. The state set up the Iowa Refugee Service Center to help the refugees. About half were resettled by the state agency and half by Catholic Social Service.

With a low state unemployment rate of 3.2 percent, the center concentrated on finding any kind of job for the refugees immediately—manual jobs, kitchen work—survival jobs. Catholic Social Service emphasized the teaching of English and vocational training, instead of immediate job placement, to help the refugees adjust in the long run. Though the two approaches conflicted, Iowans were generally proud that the state took so many refugees.

All has not been rosy between Indo-Chinese and Iowans, however. The problems in Iowa illustrate some of the weaknesses of the national resettlement program. One is isolation of the refugees from one another. U. S. immigration policy has always emphasized the adjustment of the individual and the family unit to American life. Sponsors were responsible for an individual or a family. Where possible, refugees were resettled near at least one or two other refugee families, or a group of single men might be located together. But never was a group of fifty—perhaps from the same village—placed as a unit in an American community, where they might have helped each other instead of having to depend on help from sponsors.

A moving article in *The New Yorker* early in 1980 described how a family of H'Mong—a mountain tribe from Laos—attempted suicide together after a few months in a town of 8,000 in southeast Iowa. One of the four children died before the attempt was discovered and abandoned. Four other Laotian families lived in the town, but they were from the lowlands of Laos, spoke a different language, and were not on particularly good terms with the H'Mong.

Another problem has been the large number of refugees who end up unemployed and on welfare. Colleen Shearer, the director of Iowa's center, estimates that one-third of the refugees in Iowa and one-half of all those in the United States are receiving assistance. "The domestic side of resettlement," she said, "is a shambles." The Illinois resettlement director estimated that 30 percent of Illinois's refugees are on welfare; Wisconsin reports 33 percent.

Ms. Shearer attributes the refugees' reliance on welfare to the "dumping" of the 1979 immigrants in areas where they had relatives and to the lack of adequate supervision and aid from sponsors. The refugees were encouraged to rely on welfare while learning English and training for jobs. The 1975 refugees were relatively well educated and more easily assimilated; the newer refugees were from rural areas and knew little about living in an advanced Western society.

All the Southeast Asians have experienced a severe culture shock in the United States because of the disparity between Western and Eastern cultures. American language, dress, food, and religion are foreign to them, and there were few established Indo-Chinese communities to ease the transition. The adjustment was particularly difficult for the elderly and for women, who were accustomed to meeting friends and relatives daily in the marketplace.

Adjustment was easier for children of junior high school age and younger, who learn the language quickly and pick up American ways from their schoolmates. Parents come to depend on the children to interpret for them and help them through bureaucratic procedures, but this creates tension. Western culture tends to pull children away from the family, the parents become afraid to discipline their children, and the refugees fear that "everything is out of control."

Because their culture places so much emphasis on the past, on tradition and one's ancestors, the Vietnamese seemed especially depressed. They had been cut off suddenly and reluctantly from homeland, ancestors, grandparents, and even wives and husbands. More than five hundred of the first arrivals applied to the United Nations for repatriation.

Although many 1975 arrivals have achieved a degree of material success, they have found happiness more elusive. They may own their own home, a television, and two cars, but they still experience financial worries, language problems, and homesickness. Many still think of themselves as refugees rather than immigrants, talk incessantly of going home, and are quite melancholy and fatalistic.

A young Vietnamese described his feelings about the people he works with. "I get along well with them. I feel happy, feel one of them. But at lunchtimes most of them talk about blacks and whites, say bad things. They talk about yellow people the same way. I want to be one of them, but they think other people are so low. Some days I think I won't make it. I just say, 'Forget it.' . . . Sometimes I feel like I have no soul—just a body living here. I never think about the future."

Much is known now about the economic adjustment of the first Indo-Chinese arrivals. In general, the longer they have been here the more likely they are to have a job. In January 1979 almost 58 percent of the 1975 group were employed. (This is similar to the proportion of native Americans who were employed.) In contrast, only 28 percent of the adult refugees who came in 1978 were employed. The largest number of Indo-Chinese refugees were in blue-collar jobs (45.5 percent) assembling electronic computing equipment, operating a sewing machine, handling food on an assembly line.

About 32 percent had white-collar jobs, many in education, health-related fields, or engineering.

Individual success stories abound, and certain ethnic groups fared better than others. The Tai Dam are a tribe who had migrated since 1954 to avoid the North Vietnamese. They finally moved, in 1975, to Des Moines, where they started Tai Industries, a company that produces leather key cases. They have prospered because they are energetic and "have a strong sense of how the American game is played— what is expected, what is to be done and not done." Almost 70 percent of the Tai Dam in Iowa now own their own homes.

The H'Mong, a Laotian mountain tribe, have not adapted well. Five years after settling here, they are still struggling to learn English and are living largely on welfare.

The Vietnamese in Houston have impressed the city with their energy and desire to achieve financial independence. They often work at two jobs, save their money, and share their resources with others in the extended family. An estimated 25,000 Vietnamese are in Houston, attracted by its climate, by its boom economy, by the presence of other Vietnamese. The city has a makeshift Buddhist pagoda, twenty-four-hour convenience stories with Vietnamese managers and clerks, and six columns of Nguyens in the telephone directory.

There have been conflicts, too, with Chicanos over housing in Denver, with white Americans over fishing rights in Texas. One Texas fisherman was killed in a dispute with Vietnamese refugees over the placement of crab traps off the hamlet of Seadrift, on the Gulf Coast. Americans said the Vietnamese were disregarding local customs designed to protect the shrimp crop and guarantee every fisherman's rights. Some Vietnamese pleaded ignorance of the customs and a communication problem. One hundred Vietnamese had settled in Seadrift—amounting to 10 percent of the population—and none spoke English well.

Some community officials have reported health problems among refugees: high levels of tuberculosis, parasites, and hepatitis, for example. These discoveries led to claims of inadequate screening at refugee camps.

Isolation, dependence on welfare, culture shock, and status changes, then, are some of the problems the Indo-Chinese and other refugees have faced. Studies of the 1975 immigrants reveal one primary way in which they adjusted: they moved. A significant number migrated from the first place they were settled to states with the largest concentrations of Laotians, Cambodians, or Vietnamese. Nearly one-third settled in California; 10 percent went to Texas. Large numbers settled in the Los Angeles area, in San Diego, in Houston, and in the suburbs of Washington, D. C. The original policy of dispersal was countered by the refugees themselves, who moved to be near relatives and people who spoke their language. One family who left Weatherford, Arkansas, for California explained: "The people in Weatherford were very nice, but we were the only Vietnamese family in town, so it was lonely in a way."

It is too early to tell how well the Indo-Chinese will adapt in the long run and how Americans will react to them and their culture. Their resettlement has spotlighted the entire refugee policy of the United States, however, and put into question its efficacy, as will be discussed in Chapter VIII.

OTHER ASIANS have come to the United States in less significant numbers. A steady four to five thousand Japanese have obtained immigrant visas each year since the 1950s. But many come only temporarily as representatives of businesses. Because Japan is so prosperous, the numbers are unlikely to change in the near future.

Many Iranians, classified as Asians by the Immigration and Naturalization Service, come as students. There were more students from Iran (70,000) in 1980 than from any other foreign country. They had come to schools primarily in California, Texas, and Oklahoma to obtain Western educations as part of the Shah's attempts to modernize the country. They received a large measure of attention from the public and INS when American hostages were seized in Iran in 1979. At that time President Jimmy Carter ordered that all Iranians who were here illegally be deported.

Asian immigrants will have a growing impact on American society as they continue to come in large numbers. If Cubans have transformed Miami, and if Mexican-Americans have claimed Los Angeles, Asians have added yet another dimension to the cities in which they have established communities: New York, Los Angeles, and Houston. They have generally been perceived by their neighbors as a stabilizing influence, although their influence and success in business may cause resentment. The mayor of Monterey Park, in the Los Angeles metropolitan area, describes them as a boon to his community: "They've brought in money and helped create jobs."

For the Asians themselves, the acculturation process has been slow and fraught with value clashes, generation gaps, and conflicts with other groups. They are concerned that their children, in becoming Americanized, will become bad and undisciplined. They are particularly worried by the freedom Americans have to choose their own dates and marriage partners. George Hera, a high school student, commented, "American parents, if their children want to do things, they won't stop them. But Chinese parents always want you to do the right thing."

Asians are not yet as assertive of their rights or place in American life as Hispanics have become. They have not been here as long in as large numbers, and their culture is even more of a contrast than the Hispanic. But their time is coming.

Chapter IV
THE CARIBBEANS IN NEW YORK

You always have this black thing hangin' over your head.

IMMIGRATION FROM the islands of the Caribbean—Jamaica, Barbados, Trinidad and Tobago, Haiti, and others—usually means migration to New York City. With the exception of the very poor Haitians, who head for Florida in boats, some with homemade sails, New York is the lure. There is an aura about the city that arouses the curiosity of the islanders and a determination to get there eventually. David Lawrence, a Trinidadian, talked of hearing "propaganda" about the United States such as TV advertisements showing life in California. "You hear that it's a 'hell of a place,' " he said, even though immigrants from the tropics shiver through northern winters.

The Caribbean includes Spanish-speaking Cuba and the Dominican Republic, discussed in Chapter II, and French-colonized Haiti. Most of the rest of the countries have an "Anglo" character, and their inhabitants speak British-tinged English. The Caribbean peoples to be considered in this

93

chapter—Haitians and other West Indians—are predominantly black, and New York City has been a particular goal for black immigrants. As the United States became the most cosmopolitan white nation in the world, it also became the most cosmopolitan black nation, drawing blacks from every part of the New World.

Although the numbers of West Indian immigrants have been relatively small—about 2 percent of the immigrants from 1830 to 1970—their impact on New York City has been considerable. By 1930, nearly 60 percent of the foreign black population had settled there. The city is perceived as a relatively less hostile place for blacks and as a center of popular culture, modern life-style, and social excitement. Moreover, Caribbean immigrants seem drawn to urban life. In 1976, about 67 percent of Dominicans, 66 percent of Haitians, and 53 percent of Jamaican immigrants had settled in New York. Among Caribbean peoples, only Cubans prefer Miami to New York.

The number of West Indians who immigrate is large in proportion to the size of the island populations. If we exclude Cuba and the Dominican Republic, we can estimate that immigration from the Caribbean totaled about 25,000 in 1976. That is less than from the single countries of Mexico, the Philippines, Korea, and Cuba, but greater than the legal immigration from all South America and from countries such as China and India. Of the total 5,410 were from Haiti; 9,026 from Jamaica; 4,839 from Trinidad and Tobago; and 5,805 from other West Indian countries, including Barbados.

Caribbean immigration to the United States has increased 78 percent since 1965. Like other Western Hemisphere countries close to the United States, the island nations have more immigrants who want to come than can be easily accommodated, and illegal immigration is high. The Dominican Republic, Haiti, and Jamaica are among the top fourteen source countries for illegal immigrants. Fewer former colonials are now going to Great Britain, which has been restricting immigration as the United States and Canada have been liberalizing their immigration laws.

More than curiosity attracts these immigrants. The lure of New York City is primarily economic. It is a place to earn money to make life better for dependents at home. Caribbean peoples see migration as the solution to the lack of economic opportunity at home. Colombians go to Venezuela, Mexicans go to California, and Caribbeans go to New York.

The connections have been well established. Almost every immigrant comes to join a relative, friend, or former neighbor who has sent home glowing reports and holds forth the promise of a job. Norma Beckles Rivers explained that "after you're fourteen or fifteen in my country and you really don't make it in school, that's it. Girls just get babies and stuff like that. . . . I would go back there tonight, but I cannot live the way that I'm living here." Other reasons for the movement are extreme poverty in a country such as Haiti, political instability as in Jamaica, population growth, and the availability of air travel.

The factors that make it easy for Caribbean peoples to immigrate also make it easy for them to return. More than Asians or other immigrants from far away, Caribbeans make frequent visits to the islands, and many return with an improved economic status.

Recently, however, Caribbeans have been coming north at a time of recession and high unemployment. The near bankruptcy of New York City put ethnic groups in the city in even greater competition with one another. West Indians come in with a relatively high occupational status. Nearly 20 percent are in white-collar occupations when they enter the country; they have the skills and the confidence to succeed here. They differ in their reasons for coming and in the skills they bring.

Haitians

Haitians come from the poorest Caribbean country and seem the most desperate to escape that poverty. Before the Cuban exodus in the spring of 1980 and long after boats stopped coming from Mariel, Haitians were arriving daily on the Florida coast. They came not in pleasure boats or chartered fishing boats but in leaky, makeshift sailboats jammed with men, women, and children. Vacationing sunbathers at resort beaches would look up "to see people clambering out of small boats, arriving sick, hungry, and penniless," as a newspaper reporter described it. Most brought only the clothes they were wearing.

As blacks, the Haitians receive a mixed welcome. Miami is a city that has already absorbed tens of thousands of Cubans, Nicaraguans, and Haitians but has been unable to provide decent jobs and housing for its native black population. The Haitians' rural origins and uncertain legal status make their adjustment even more difficult.

Haitians are the most recent group to immigrate in large numbers to the United States. The movement to New York began to increase significantly after 1965. Most of the 5,000 Haitians who come legally each year come to New York. An equal number come illegally to New York or overstay tourist visas. By unofficial estimates, there are now about 300,000 Haitians in the New York metropolitan area.

With a long waiting list for visas and increasingly skeptical consular officials, it has become more and more difficult for a Haitian to come legally. Many came in the early 1970s with Department of Labor certification to fill jobs as dress-makers or shoemakers for which they were needed. Now the main preference categories available are as relatives of citizens or permanent residents. A tourist visa may require a bribe of about $1,500 to a U. S. consular official, one immigrant reports.

Faced with the difficulty of coming legally, more Haitians seem to be opting for the 700-mile journey to Miami, perilous as it may be. Boat traffic to Florida began as a trickle in 1972, then increased fairly rapidly in the late 1970s. In 1978, some 1,810 arrived on the Florida coast; in 1979 the number was 2,522; and by August of 1980, more than 4,800 had already come. On any single day a hundred or more new Haitians may disperse into Dade County, the southeastern county in which Miami lies.They arrive without visas or any legal permission to immigrate. Some disembark at night to avoid immigration authorities.

One young man described a twenty-two-day trip on a boat so crowded with 140 people that he couldn't move. It reminded him of a movie he had seen about slave trafficking in the eighteenth century. The food on the boat ran out, then the water; one passenger starved to death. Often there are drowning deaths as well when a boat capsizes or sinks.

Why risk such a life-threatening journey? Clearly, Haitians are being pushed by desperate conditions. Some claim to be political refugees, but most come looking for jobs. Haiti is the poorest country in the Western Hemisphere and one of the most impoverished in the world. The average Haitian can expect to earn $212 a year and to live for only fifty-two years. Of every 1,000 infants born in Haiti, 150 die within the first year of life. Half of all adults have no wage-earning jobs at all and subsist on what they can grow or find.

"It was awful in Haiti," one arrival said. He was always

hungry. "I'd prefer to stay in jail in Miami for ten years than go back to Haiti," another said. "I had all kinds of problems at home—no food, no money, no work. It was miserable. I had to leave."

Many immigrants come from the poor, drought-scorched northwestern region of Haiti. About 80 percent of the Haitian population lives in rural areas where most own land to farm. But population growth, drought, and the division and subdivision of family farms over the years have brought about the current economic plight.

Haiti has been ruled by the dictators of the Duvalier family. After "Papa Doc" died in 1971, Haitians expected some liberalization under his son Jean-Claude. But an opposition political party and human rights rallies were short-lived. Duvalier's life-style is in stark contrast to the poverty of the majority. His wedding in 1980 cost between three and five million dollars.

Many Haitians emigrated first to the Bahamas, which look on the map like stepping stones from Haiti to Florida. They were welcomed during boom years in the Bahamas because they filled a need for cheap labor. But in 1978 unemployment began to rise and the government launched "Operation Clean-up" to expel 400 Haitians a month. Faced with a forced return to Haiti, many set sail for Florida instead, and 600 arrived on the coast in June 1978, the first month of the operation.

As the Bahamas repatriated Haitians, the United States tried to decide what to do with the newcomers. In the mid-1970s Haitians who arrived without visas were questioned and detained. Many spent several months in prison waiting to be deported. Others were released and faded out of sight of the authorities. By September 1978, nearly 10,000 had applied for political asylum. Only 58 had received it; more than

200 had returned voluntarily; and 181 had been deported. It became obvious that deciding each Haitian's application individually would take years.

At that point the State Department sent a study team to Haiti to find out if returnees were indeed imprisoned, tortured, or harassed. The team could find only 86 of the 600 returnees they sought, but from those few interviews they "uncovered no significant indication of mistreatment or of punishment of returnees." The team concluded that the Haitians had left entirely for economic reasons.

Haitians in the United States responded with a lawsuit. Lawyers for the Haitians contended that "the majority have fled Haiti not because of poverty but rather because of political repression." They cited other investigations that had uncovered some evidence of arrests, torture, beatings, and mysterious disappearances.

As the arguments proceeded in court, the Carter administration looked for a way to solve the dilemma the Haitian influx presented for U. S. immigration policy. Both Cubans and Haitians arrived in southern Florida in the spring of 1980, but they were received very differently. The Cubans had long been regarded as political refugees. In the 1960s and 1970s they fit the definition of a refugee as someone fleeing a communist dictatorship. The 1980 Cuban refugees, by contrast, seemed to be coming for economic reasons as well. Crop failures and food shortages had prompted some to leave, they admitted. But they, too, were welcomed at first with open arms.

Haitians, coming from a country with a right-wing dictatorship, did not fit the traditional definition of refugees. And, argued Miami INS director Raymond A. Morris, "If we're going to let Haitians in because they're hungry, then how can we stop people from India, Southeast Asia, and

China from coming in?" The Haitians were detained at first and given very little government help. They were eligible for food stamps, free physical examinations, social counseling, and sometimes work permits. But most were not allowed to work and were left to fend for themselves and find charity where they could, mainly from members of the black community in Miami.

The contrast raised charges of racism in U. S. immigration policy. President Carter had been willing to use emergency powers to admit the 3,500 Cubans who sought asylum in the Peruvian embassy in Havana. Black leaders, especially members of the Congressional Black Caucus, urged that Haitians be granted refuge as a group, too. "If the Haitians were white and were coming from a communist country, there's no question the American government would grant them asylum," a lawyer said.

Another issue was cost. Local governments claimed they should be reimbursed for the cost of helping Haitians and Cubans. If immigrants are categorized as refugees, they are eligible for more benefits, particularly welfare and Medicaid. Per capita grants are also given to sponsors for each refugee they resettle. The decision on the status of the two thus had financial as well as legal ramifications.

Finally, in June 1980, the administration decided to give Cubans and Haitians a new status as "special entrants." Those already here could stay for six months until Congress could consider their status more completely. After two years they could become permanent residents. As a result of this decision, Haitians became eligible for welfare and medical assistance. Carter also asked Congress to reimburse state and local governments for their expenses in providing medical assistance, special education, and social services to the refugees for one year.

Meanwhile, a federal judge ruled that the Immigration and Naturalization Service had violated the rights of the Haitians it sought to deport and must reconsider their asylum claims.

Thus the Haitians already here have gained a more secure status and will probably be allowed to stay. But those who arrived after June 1980 and want to stay may be required to prove a "well-founded fear" of persecution if they returned. As the Bahamas continued to force them out, Haitians were arriving in Florida at the rate of about 200 a day in the fall of 1980.

Once here, even legally, Haitians have had a hard time acclimatizing themselves. They are mainly poor, rural, unskilled, illiterate, non-English-speaking, and insecure in their status. But economic necessity forces the adjustment. A Haitian's first task, like any immigrant's, is to find a job. Most begin at the lowest levels: as migrant workers, citrus pickers, maids, waitresses, seamstresses, baby-sitters. For those who immigrated legally in 1976 the largest occupational category was "operatives," machine operators in factories. Despite holding jobs that pay low wages, the Haitians are hardworking and frugal and manage to support relatives in Haiti. In 1977 immigrants sent an estimated $83 million to Haiti from the United States.

Another big problem is language. About 95 percent of Haitians speak only Creole, a language derived from African, European, and Arawak Indian elements. From 2 to 5 percent of the population speak fluent French, the official language of Haiti and the language of the elite. Very few Haitians are literate in either language.

The health of the Haitians is generally poor. They are fifteen times more likely to have tuberculosis than other members of the Dade County (Miami) community. About one in four adults has syphilis. Malnutrition, anemia, yaws, parastitic infestations, hypertension, and low levels of immunization are also common. Largely because of fear of being deported, mental health may be a problem, too. Many Haitians avoid all contact with authorities, hiding for weeks in New York apartments and greatly overestimating the ability of INS to track them down.

Haitians have clustered in two areas: the New York City metropolitan area and Dade County, Florida. The New York Haitian community is somewhat older and more firmly established, and its members are better able to help new arrivals. One woman told of her first job cutting up chickens in a factory in Brooklyn. When she began working there in 1970 she was one of only three Haitians; the other two were a husband and wife. "They brought plenty Haitians," she said. When she left five years later, about a hundred were working there.

The Haitians in New York represent all classes, from the French-speaking, educated elite to the poor farmers. Most are unskilled laborers who earn average weekly wages of $150 or less. They must adjust not only to a different culture but to life in one of the largest cities in the world and to phenomena such as escalators, and doors that open by themselves, and locking doors. Haitians in New York have established some social and religious associations—Catholic churches, a weekly newspaper, a Carib folkloric dance troupe, and a day-care center.

Haitians in Miami live a more precarious life. As they arrive, the local community is hard put to provide food and housing. The county has spent about $1.7 million a year for social services, primarily medical services. Burdine's department store provided daily food for 100 Haitians for a time; a Baptist church opened its doors and provided food and a place to sleep. But malnutrition, unemployment, and overcrowded housing persist. Most Haitians have settled in the inner city, in a poor, run-down section of dilapidated wooden bungalows now known as Little Haiti. A survey showed that 41 percent of Haitians in Miami cannot find work and that more than 60 percent earn less than $114 a week.

Unlike many other Western Hemisphere immigrants, most Haitians plan to stay here. They feel they have no choice. "What I'm going to do if I go back to Haiti?" a housekeeper and baby-sitter asked and then answered, "Nothing." People can't find wage-paying jobs in Haiti, another woman said, and the situation is getting worse.

Many immigrants fondly recall living in a climate that is 80 degrees year round, being able to leave doors open, and putting in easier workdays with long breaks for lunch. But they also seem to have little optimism that the problems of Haiti will be solved quickly enough to benefit them.

Jamaicans and Other West Indians

Emigration from the other Caribbean countries—Jamaica, Barbados, Trinidad and Tobago, the Bahamas—has not been so strongly propelled by poor economies and repressive governments. But emigration fluctuates as conditions change in these countries.

Jamaica, for example, experienced a period of political instability and violence in the late 1970s and early 1980s. More than five hundred people were killed in 1980 as elections approached. Residents sent money out of the country; education, careers, and property were threatened. Under a left-leaning government unemployment reached 30 percent and the foreign debt was $1 billion. Under these conditions, as much as 1 percent of Jamaica's population was leaving. Each year 9,000 came to the United States.

Jamaican laborers have often come temporarily to cut

sugarcane for five months at a time in Florida. But recent immigrants have been professionals, technicians, managers, and administrators, those the country can least afford to lose. An estimated 200,000 Jamaicans live in New York and 95,000 in the rest of the country, including some 40,000 in south Florida.

By contrast, the islands of Trinidad and Tobago off the coast of Venezuela are benefiting from oil discoveries, and emigration may slacken. Five thousand a year have been coming to the United States. About 250,000 Barbadians and their descendants also live in New York City, as do smaller numbers from the Bahamas, Granada, and other islands.

CARIBBEAN IMMIGRATION has continued in the pattern of earlier decades. New York City is more than ever the North American mecca. The West Indian carnival in Brooklyn each summer attracts thousands and has become an entrenched ethnic event like the Saint Patrick's Day and Columbus Day parades for the Irish and Italians.

West Indians continue to prosper in New York. The 1970 census showed they achieve a higher occupational status and income in New York City than American blacks do. They have a psychological advantage, coming from societies where blacks are a majority. They don't expect race to be a barrier. As immigrants they are also more willing to work in low-status jobs and save for the long run. They have an advantage over some immigrants, in that they speak English.

West Indians do encounter racial discrimination, however. "You always have this black thing hangin' over your head," a Trinidadian commented. Compared with white ethnic groups in income and upward mobility, West Indians tend to be at the median level or lower.

One of the reasons West Indians have prospered in New York City, despite racial discrimination, is that they attract black customers to their businesses. They open grocery stores, tailor shops, jewelry stores, fruit stands, and real estate offices in the ghettos and compete with white businesses. West Indians have been successful politically, too, using the black community as an electoral base. Shirley Chisholm and Stokely Carmichael are in this tradition.

New York and other cities, such as Los Angeles, increasingly have large non-white populations as a result of the urban migration of southern blacks and the immigration of Mexicans, Puerto Ricans, and West Indians. This promotes a certain ethnic cosmopolitanism that is beneficial to the immigrant. Caribbean peoples regard themselves as cosmopolitan. Describing her native Trinidad, an immigrant said, "You sit there with Indians, and you sit with Chinese children, and you sit there with so-called Trinidad white people, and you never have a problem! You never *think* about it bein' a problem, because you are in this little country. When you come abroad, it takes awhile for you to see certain things."

Many West Indians see the public schools as inadequate, especially in discipline, as compared with the British system in the islands. "I was very much surprised that the standard of education was so low among black people," a woman commented, "because in Trinidad, they tend to give you a British education, which covers everything from A to Z." West Indians share many of the values of the Protestant ethic. They emphasize education, ambition, hard work, saving, and investment. But they also have ethnic pride and bring a certain gentleness, a soft-spoken quality that is rare in the city.

Adjusting to city life is not easy. New York winters are a far cry from those in the tropics, and living in a closed-up apartment building is a new experience. "In the winter the windows were closed all the time. I wasn't used to that," said David Lawrence, a Trinidadian. "Even the building blocks in Trinidad have holes in them; windows are always open. I had to adjust to being enclosed; it drove me up the wall."

David Lawrence is a West Indian with one foot in each of two cultures. He came to New York City in 1977 at age nineteen. His mother had worked eight years as a baby-sitter and had brought her five sons into the United States under the relative-preference category. After scoring well on a test, Lawrence was offered a job as a community-service officer with the housing police, working in a housing project in the Brownsville area of Brooklyn. He has since been promoted.

Lawrence says that his Trinidadian education has been an advantage in the United States: "A lot of people I run into, on the job and off, are not really illiterate but not well educated either." He goes to college in the evenings, hoping to develop a career in law enforcement or become a lawyer.

Lawrence is eligible to train to be a state trooper, but he would first have to become a citizen. Becoming a citizen and staying are decisions he isn't ready to make. Lawrence cites the laxity of American society, the lack of respect for older people, drugs that "you can buy on the street like candy," teenage pregnancies, and the number of handguns around as problems he sees here.

By contrast, Lawrence remembers a childhood that was "really beautiful" and close to nature. At home "you could just lay around and look at the stars all night and just drift away. . . . In the city, you hardly see stars at night." If he could make enough money to be comfortable, have an education, own a home, raise a family, give his children an education, and still be able to travel back and forth to Trinidad occasionally, he would stay.

Lawrence is a West Indian with an appreciation of both worlds who is temporarily committed to neither. He illustrates how immigration to the United States has become an essential part of life for a significant number of West Indians. Caribbean immigration to New York has also spurred the reverse trend—a return to the islands. Americans have long been attracted to the Caribbean for vacations, retirement, investment, and escape from U. S. taxes or even prosecution. Money and a home in the sun seem an ideal combination to West Indians, too, even if getting it means a temporary stay in New York City slums.

Chapter V
THE OLDEST IMMIGRANTS

Falling into a honey nest?

THE DAYS when Europeans left for the New World in droves are over. The New World seems less new and inviting now, and life at home has improved. But a steady stream continues from the countries that have always sent immigrants: Italy, Germany, England, and Ireland. And immigration has increased from a few others, such as Portugal, Greece and the Soviet Union.

European immigration has been eclipsed by Asian and Western Hemisphere immigration in the last twenty years. After 1789 Europe and Canada contributed 85 percent of the immigrants to the United States, but that situation changed when European and Canadian economies improved and the 1965 amendments opened immigration to all nationalities. Only one-fifth of the newest immigrants are from Europe. Only the United Kingdom remains among the top eight sending countries. Only four European countries—Germany, Italy, Portugal, and Great Britain—have sent more than 10,000 in any year since 1965.

As European immigration declined, the second- and third-generation descendants of earlier immigrants were coming of age. Their forebears were the turn-of-the-century immigrants from southern and eastern Europe. The 1924 national-origins law was aimed at these nationalities, and their immigrating numbers were reduced from 1924 to 1965. After years of restriction there was a temporary surge from these countries in the late 1960s, swelling to 20,000 or more for Italy and Portugal. But since the 1970s, southern and eastern European immigration has stayed at a few thousand a year.

The Europeans who immigrate now come for carefully considered reasons. A young British doctor comes because he has grown tired of waiting for a prestigious consultancy position in the British national health system. A Soviet Jewish scientist leaves because his opportunities to do research in his field have been curtailed. A Czechoslovakian tennis player defects because she will have more professional freedom and greater earnings here. An Italian comes to join his brother, who says his carpentry skills are in demand.

Many, like the Greeks and Portuguese Azoreans, are still economic exiles. Others, particularly the Italians, are predominantly "recalls"—relatives of American citizens. Large numbers from all countries are needed workers—professionals, technicians, and craftsmen. And there are political refugees, particularly from Russia and the communist eastern European nations. Soviet Jews and eastern Europeans constitute the third largest group of recent refugees, after Cubans and Indo-Chinese. A few nationality groups will be used to illustrate the categories of economic exile, recall, needed worker, and refugee.

What has happened with Italian immigration in recent years is indicative of the reasons for the decline in European immigration. Prior to 1965 Italy had an annual quota of 6,000. Under pressure that number was repeatedly increased until it stood at over 20,000. When the 1965 amendments provided a wider opening, about 25,000 Italians were admitted each year until 1968. Most of the immigrants were economic exiles.

Suddenly, however, Italian immigration began to decline. In 1974 only 15,000 came; in 1976 only about 8,000. The reasons for the decline stem mainly from conditions in Italy. After years of emigrating to escape poverty and unemployment, Italians began to solve their problems at home. Trade unions were strengthened, more clerical jobs became available, and Italian workers looked for work in Europe instead of abroad. For the first time one year in the late 1970s, more Italians returned to Italy than left. If a hundred Italians do leave to find work, eighty of them now look elsewhere in Europe, and only twenty of the emigrants come to the United States.

Most of those immigrating to the United States are joining relatives. Occupationally almost 40 percent are professionals, technicians, and kindred workers. Italians have also responded to an increase demand here for carpenters, tailors, steel workers, welders, plumbers, and electricians. More than half settle in twelve American cities, with New York, Philadelphia, and Boston leading the list.

As Italian immigration declined in the 1970s, immigration remained strong from Greece and Portugal, two countries where economic factors still push people to emigrate. Portuguese immigration has been especially high from the economically depressed Azores, nine islands southwest of Portugal. Portugal has ranked fifth, sixth, or seventh as a

An ocean-going tugboat packed with close to 900 Cuban refugees coming into Key West in May, 1980.

Vietnamese refugees debarking from a jet that brought them from Malaysia to Los Angeles International Airport, in 1979. Mostly ethnic Chinese, the refugees were to be located to various parts of the country by church groups.

A Czechoslovakian woman immigrant, arriving at Kennedy airport in New York, is welcomed to America by her grand niece.

A family of illegal aliens being processed for their return to Mexico by a border patrol agent in San Ysidro, California.

The oath of citizenship being taken by 720 immigrants at a naturalization ceremony in Boston's Faneuil Hall.

source country for immigrants, sending more than 10,000 a year.

Most Azoreans find blue-collar jobs here, some working on farms or in the mills of Fall River, Massachusetts, and Providence, Rhode Island, where the Portuguese first settled in the early 1900s. Many Portuguese women are skilled needleworkers and are in great demand in the textile and garment industries.

Greeks come as craftsmen, carpenters, jewelers, bakers, and sailors. Once here they often work in service industries and as bartenders, ushers, and hairdressers. Over 40 percent of the new Greek immigrants settle in New York City.

More Greeks than any other nationality also jump ship in U. S. ports. In fact, 2,499 did so in 1971, twice the number who remained when ships from the Western Hemisphere left. One primary motivation of ship jumpers is to avoid Greek military service.

Once here, Greeks have been slow to reach out of their close-knit communities to the surrounding society. They tend to be suspicious of outsiders, a cultural trait that was a mode of survival in Greece. Greek children are often shy and withdrawn in school and restricted at home. Only about 4 percent of non-English-speaking Greek children are in bilingual programs, in contrast to widespread programs for Spanish speakers. Greeks have been a migratory people, and many do not intend to stay. Only about 5 percent reach the goal of making enough money to return home a success, however.

Thus Italians, Portuguese, and Greeks come as economic exiles and relatives of citizens, but many are also needed workers for the United States. Along with skilled workers, European professionals have been attracted to the United States. In fact, the brain drain began in the 1960s as a European phenomenon but Europeans were soon surpassed by immigrating professionals from less developed countries. Some European countries continue to experience brain drain. Britons, especially, have constituted 5 percent of all immigrants to the United States in the professionals-technicians-kindred workers category in recent years. Russia and Canada, too, rank below four Asian countries in the number of professionals and kindred workers sent.

The last category of European immigrant—the political refugee—is a member of the most exotic group. The 1965 definition of "refugee" was modeled on the Hungarian freedom fighter and the Czechoslovakian fleeing Russian tanks. Today the refugees are dissidents and Jews leaving Russia itself, and occasional daring escapees, like the Rumanians who flew a state-owned crop-dusting plane across Hungary to Austria in the summer of 1980.

Except for periods of political upheaval, it has been quite difficult for Europeans under communist governments to emigrate. A few hundred Rumanians may be granted permission to leave each year to join family in the United States. Russia has allowed some people, mainly Jews, to leave. A fairly large number of Poles have managed to immigrate, legally and illegally, especially to Chicago and Detroit.

The largest group of recent refugees from Europe has been made up of Soviet Jews. In 1968 the Soviet Union began allowing a few Jews to leave each year, ostensibly to go to Israel. More than 3,000 left in 1969 and 34,000 each in 1972 and 1973. The flow peaked at 51,000 in 1979. Of those who left, 20 percent eventually ended up in the United States, many going to Israel or the Netherlands first. In 1980 the number began to decline, but in that ten-year period, about 70,000 Soviet Jews had settled in the United States.

Jews wanted to leave, some because they were attracted to Israel and others because they sensed a growing anti-Semitism in the U.S.S.R. and a reduction in career and educational opportunities for Jews. Religious education has been forbidden in the Soviet Union, and most Jews have grown up without practicing their religion. "I tell you the truth, Russian people of our generation aren't religious," an immigrant in New York said. The Jews did not live badly in Russia, but many were beginning to fear their children would be denied a university education.

Why Russia allowed the exodus is unclear. It was partly encouraged by the atmosphere of detente and partly by the sit-down strikes and mass meetings of those who wanted to leave. By 1979, when 4,000 a month were leaving the Soviet Union, the United States felt pressure to admit more refugees than was customary. This, along with the Indo-Chinese exodus, prompted the Refugee Act of 1980.

The Soviet Jews who immigrated came mainly to Boston and New York. In New York at least half settled in Brooklyn, particularly in the neighborhood of Brighton Beach, known as Little Odessa by the Sea. One-third or more of its residents come from that Black Sea port in the Ukraine.

The Russians find life in a capitalist society somewhat overwhelming at first. They are amazed by the supermarkets and department stores but disoriented when they must compete for a job instead of being assigned one. They have never before had to find their own apartment, look for a better job, or choose a doctor or school. They are anxious about taking a first job for which they are overqualified, since they are not accustomed to the idea of upward mobility. People are slotted into jobs in Russia more or less permanently.

At least 30 percent of the Soviet Jews who came here in the last ten years are university graduates. Many end up driving taxis, however, until they can learn English and pass licensing exams in their professions. Engineers, chemists, machinists, tool-and-die makers, computer experts, draftsmen, musicians, and artists find appropriate work more easily than doctors, teachers, lawyers, or social workers. Writers and poets find the adjustment particularly hard. For all, the adjustment is painful at times. "They hear it's so good here, they think they're falling into a honey nest," said a staff member of the Hebrew Immigrant Aid Society. Getting the knack of capitalism, however, takes awhile.

The exodus of Jews fell steadily in 1980 for several reasons. Soviet visa officials were preoccupied with preparations for the Olympics, emigration was restricted in retaliation for trade cutbacks after the Soviets had invaded Afghanistan, and many urban areas began to feel the economic consequences of the emigration of well-educated Jews. When another large group will immigrate is a matter of Soviet policy rather than of U. S. immigration law.

Further European immigration in the last quarter of the twentieth century is likely to be selective, occurring when there are political upheavals or in response to specific U. S. labor needs. A constant small stream of migration both ways is bound to continue.

The new arrivals are refreshing the white ethnic communities in which they settle—communities that have only recently gained a measure of acceptance in American society. The Slovaks, Poles, Greeks, and Italians, among others, became more assertive of their rights and cultural identities in the 1960s, as other minorities were demanding attention to theirs. Thus the newest arrivals have the support of communities that have established themselves in the mainstream. They are now more often identified by religion or status— white Catholics, Jews, blue-collar workers—than by nationality.

The acculturation of the earlier European immigrants has not been totally successful, sometimes by choice. The adjectives "forgotten" or "neglected" are often used to describe white ethnics. Whereas media and government attention has focused on blacks or Hispanics, many elderly white ethnics live in poverty and without social services. Fewer second-generation white ethnics attend college than do Asians, Hispanics, and West Indians.

The Canadians

Canadians hardly seem like immigrants to the United States. Crossing the northern border hardly seems like leaving one country for another. Nor is it an irrevocable act, whichever direction the traveler is going. Yet numerically immigration from Canada has been significant. Historically about twice as many Canadians as Mexicans have come to the United States—four million compared with two million. And native-born Canadians have always outnumbered native-born Mexicans in the U. S. Census. Some 800,000 lived here in 1970, as compared with 750,000 Mexicans.

Though numerous, Canadians are not very noticeable. They are similar to Americans in appearance, culture, and language, except for those who are from French-speaking areas. Mainly because of the constant possibility of returning, Canadians are much less likely than other immigrants to become U. S. citizens. Whereas one-third of all immigrants from 1966 and 1970 were naturalized within five years, only one-seventh of Canadians were.

Since 1965 Canadian immigration has dropped 80 percent, from 38,327 to 7,638. The change has been a reaction not to U. S. law but to changes in Canada. The economy has improved, especially for the middle classes, and a sense of

Canadian identity is growing. There may also be a reluctance to become involved in U. S. problems. A reverse migration of Americans to Canada was strong in the late 1960s and early 1970s as draft resisters sought a haven there. Canada's immigration law has recently become more restrictive, selecting immigrants according to a point system.

As Canadian immigration declined, Canada itself, because of the open border, became a conduit for illegal immigrants from other nations who wanted to come to the United States. Many would-be immigrants fly to Montreal or Toronto and then make their way south.

Africans and Others

Africans have never immigrated to the United States in large numbers, except by force. The geographic and psychological distances are great, and the reputation of the United States on race is also a deterrent. A trickle may be forming from West Africa, however. In Nigeria, 400 U. S. visas are granted each day. There are more than 20,000 Nigerian students in the United States, almost all of whom return to Nigeria's booming economy.

The United States also seems to have become a haven for the wealthy, or at least for their money. Wealthy Arabs, Latin Americans, and deposed dictators send their money and their families, and they themselves come, when pressed. One provision of the immigration law until 1978 was known as the "foreign investor provision." It granted a visa number to any foreign investor willing to put $40,000 into an American business and then hire at least one worker who was a U. S. citizen. The economic advantage to the United States was obvious, but the law allowed immigrants to buy their way in. No investor numbers have been granted for the past two years.

No BOOK on immigration gives a complete picture unless it mentions emigration, the flow of people out of a country. No data have been collected on emigration since the 1950s, but estimates based on census data have been made. They show that 1.1 million of the foreign-born and an additional 385,000 American citizens left the United States between 1960 and 1970.

The citizens went to Canada, Australia, and Belgium, predominantly. Among them were draft resisters (before the draft was abolished), literary expatriates, wealthy Americans evading taxes, and some, like Robert Vesco, evading legal prosecution. Others are in search of opportunity elsewhere. For many of the foreign-born, returning home marks the end of the American dream and a failure in the acculturation process, the topic of the next chapter.

Chapter VI

THE MELTING
EXPERIENCE

It's equal opportunity.

ONCE HERE, the newest immigrants go through the same adjustment earlier immigrants did, but the pace seems faster now. They must give up some of the ways of their native country and adopt American ways if they are to survive and thrive. Many of the newest immigrants interviewed were keenly aware of what they have sacrificed to immigrate. Some—like Tieng Huynh—did not leave by choice and left family behind. Others, like a Haitian teacher turned housekeeper, would prefer to have stayed in their native countries if they could have found jobs. The more optimistic, such as Erlinda Nool and David Lawrence, feel they still have the option of returning.

One's feelings about being an immigrant affect the adjustment he or she makes to the new culture. An immigrant may thrive on the change or become severely depressed. On the whole the newest immigrants have a strong track record

123

economically. Yet, many find that the price of economic success is high. As they achieve materialistic goals, they must adjust socially, culturally, and personally as well. That is often a far more difficult task.

Vietnamese Tieng Huynh is a financial success in the United States. He lives in a well-furnished, fairly modern apartment. He feels lucky about his job because he is becoming more skilled and experienced. But he feels at times like a body without a soul. "People think I am happy. I have money, car, nice apartment, too," he said, "but my head is all messed up."

This chapter will look first at the economic adjustment immigrants make and at their economic impact on American society. (The economic impact of illegal immigrants will be considered in more detail in Chapter VII.) Then the chapter will look at the overall acculturation process, how immigrants adjust socially and culturally, what changes they make in life-style and values, and what changes, if any, American society makes in response to them. It will look at the special problems of refugees. It will touch briefly, too, on the political involvement of immigrants, on the phenomenon of commuting, and on bilingualism.

Economic Impact

Two recent immigrants present their views on jobs:

"People talk about the boat people taking Americans' jobs," a Vietnamese refugee said, "and I feel bad; I'm one of them. But then I say, 'Look, I'm a single guy; I pay 40 percent in taxes.' "

"I've heard the statement that the immigrant is taking a job away from a native," Trinidadian David Lawrence says, and he adds that he felt some resentment from his fellow employees, American blacks, when he was promoted, but he doesn't think the statement is true. "It's equal opportunity; they took the same exam I did to get the job; I did better on it."

In the past, immigrants were an economic asset to the United States. Large numbers of people were needed to populate the land, to clear and farm it, to work on the railroads and in the mines, to work in factories in the cities. But by the last quarter of the twentieth century, the concept of a forever-expanding economy has faded. One hears talk of scarce resources and limited growth, and the question of whether the United States still needs immigrants.

Yet jobs remain the great lure for immigrants. Mexicans, Haitians, and Filipinos alike come here looking for work, and generally they find it. The jobs they take fall into several categories:

1. *Jobs nobody else wants.* These are low-paying, low-status jobs that Americans turn up their noses at: washing dishes in a restaurant, sewing garments in a factory or at home (piecework), taking care of young children in their home, cleaning house, moving household goods, parking cars. Immigrants take these jobs either as a matter of survival or because even the low wages look good in comparison to what they earned at home. Or they see the jobs as only temporary, the first step up the economic ladder.

2. *Seasonal agricultural work.* Although agriculture is now largely mechanized, some crops must still be picked by hand. This requires laborers who will appear to pick for only a few weeks and then move on. Few American families can tolerate such a haphazard life, but the foreign laborer stays as long as the

work lasts and then returns home. Agricultural jobs represent a declining share of the jobs sought by legal and illegal immigrants, however.

3. *Professional and technical jobs.* The United States does not train enough natives in fields such as health and the sciences, so that jobs are available to those trained abroad.

4. *Small entrepreneurships.* Immigrants who can master the free enterprise system can create their own jobs. Chinese laundries and West Indian tailor shops, Greek restaurants and Korean fruit and vegetable stands give evidence that opening a small business is the goal for some and the last resort for others.

By and large, immigrants do find jobs. If they didn't, the word would spread to other potential immigrants.

The question of whether immigrants take jobs away from natives is more complicated, however. Growers argue that immigrants take jobs that would otherwise go unfilled. They say they cannot find native workers when they need them. Yet there are indications that immigrants do compete for jobs with the unskilled or least-skilled American workers, particularly with minorities and teenagers, who have high unemployment rates. The unemployment rate for black teenagers was 39.3 percent in 1980. In Texas, along the Mexican border, the unemployment rate is twice the rate in the state as a whole.

Illegal aliens, especially, are resented. "There are many black teenagers who would like to have some of the jobs these illegal aliens are taking," an INS investigator in New York said. Cesar Chavez complains that illegal aliens fill about 20 percent of the farm jobs in California and do all the potato harvesting in Idaho. On the other hand, economists maintain that there will always be unemployment of about 3.5 percent because a certain number of people are just not interested in working.

The native worker has some advantages over the immigrant in competing for a job. He or she speaks English, has some education, has family and friends to help, and is relatively settled here. The immigrant, however, may have the advantage of being more aggressive, less fatalistic, and more willing to work unceasingly in the short run. Immigrant communities often have their own job-information network. "They've got the greatest grapevine in the world," one immigration official said. "A week off the plane they're holding down one or two jobs and working Sundays and nights. You have to remember why they came."

The competition for jobs has been obvious in some areas, in disputes between Vietnamese and natives over fishing rights in the Gulf of Mexico, between legal and illegal Mexican workers in California, and between Cubans and native blacks in Miami. The new wave of Cuban immigrants in 1980 sharpened the competition and was a contributing factor in the spring riot. "The Latin community is being developed and a lot of money is being poured into it by government agencies," a black real estate man said, "but the black community is treated like the stepchild."

The 1980 unemployment rate in Dade County for whites, including Hispanics, was 8 percent; for blacks, it was 17 percent. Furthermore, 38 percent of blacks in Dade County live below the poverty level, compared with 18 percent of Hispanics and 10 percent of non-Hispanic whites. Miami's commercial connection with Latin America also put blacks at a disadvantage by making bilingualism a requirement for many jobs.

Among professionals the element of competition between natives and immigrants is less direct. Few trained physicians go without work in the United States. But the struggle for entry into U. S. medical schools eliminates many aspiring doctors. Only about 6,000 black doctors were practicing in the United States in 1970, but 7,000 Flipino doctors, who had obtained their training abroad, were licensed to practice here.

Some economists argue that the major economic impact of immigrants, especially of illegal aliens, is not competition for jobs. It is the newcomers' desperate willingness to work that holds down wages for all workers. If a Haitian seamstress will accept 75¢ for sewing a dress, why pay someone else a dollar?

Even a temporary immigrant-worker program may hold down wages and take jobs away from natives. The bracero program imported cheap Mexican labor during the 1940s, 1950s, and 1960s. In the cucumber industry in Michigan most of the pickers were Mexican. Farmers there claimed U. S. workers would not pick cucumbers. But when the bracero program ended in 1964, wages increased, working conditions improved, and U. S. workers became available. The price of cucumbers went up, too. Thus immigrant workers may displace natives by working for lower wages than an American feels is worthwhile. This benefits the general population because it keeps prices lower, but it does not help the native worker who loses earnings.

Overall, however, the economic impact of immigrants is seen as favorable. An economist at the University of Illinois at Champaign-Urbana concluded after a study that "the average immigrant is a remarkably good investment for taxpayers." From two to six years after entering the country, the average immigrant family earns about as much as the average native family. After six years it earns more. (Immigrants tend to be young, of working age, and have few children when they arrive. Among native families are many who are retired and receiving Social Security.) Nor do the newcomers use welfare or unemployment compensation heavily. A General Accounting Office study of immigrants who had been in the United States less than five years revealed that only about 3 percent were receiving Supplemental Security Income.

One economic adjustment many immigrants make is that women begin to take jobs outside the home, something they may not have done before. The work of immigrant women in child care enables more native women to take jobs, too.

Another facet of the economic impact of immigrants is the amount of money they send home. Mexicans send as much as $3 billion annually, but they spend much of their income here, too. They have already paid taxes on the money sent abroad and some of it is ultimately used to buy goods and services from the United States. The amount of money sent home is a testament to the frugality and hard work of immigrants and to the vast disparity between incomes in the United States and those in Third World countries.

In sum, the United States benefits economically from immigrants because they provide a cheap supply of labor, the professionals and technicians among them fill in where there are shortages, and they create jobs through their own enterprises. The adverse effects are primarily on the minorities and unskilled workers with whom they compete. As a result, although the population as a whole seems to welcome immigrants, there is a heightened awareness of scarce resources and possible ethnic conflicts in times of economic hardship.

Acculturation

After the first few years, when immigrants' income is well established, their goals become less immediate and more elusive. Immigrants usually want to become more a part of American society, to feel better about themselves, to regain some of the status and sense of self-worth that they lost in the immigration process. Once having become self-sufficient, the immigrant is encouraged to "melt," to become that ill-defined individual—an American.

American immigration history long emphasized the idea of the melting pot. As early as 1782 J. Hector St. John Crève-coeur wrote in *Letters from an American Farmer* that "here individuals of all nations are melted into a new race of men, whose labours and posterity will one day cause great changes in the world." Here was not only a land of economic opportunity but a land where the individual differences that divide the nationalities of the world would melt and be subsumed in one harmonious nation of free people. Here a person could shed an old self and become new.

For a long time, too, the dominant Anglo-Saxon culture was seen as superior. Immigrants were expected to strive to be like Anglo-Saxons and to discard their own ethnic characteristics. They were expected to be assimilated into the American scene. How this melting process was to be achieved was always something of a mystery. Intermarriage with a native, of course, would be the ultimate assimilation.

Americans have viewed assimilation as a process an individual goes through. As in the resettlement of the Indo-Chinese refugees, help is given to individuals, not to groups. The strongest personalities are expected to succeed. Those who want to be assimilated, however, find the process difficult. To abandon homeland, family, roots, and tradition and to replace them with a new identity is a wrenching experience. Nor is it necessarily the best goal for an immigrant.

More recently, the immigrant has been recognized as a member of a group with its own culture. Sociologists emphasize that immigrants acculturate as a group; one culture blends with another and a sharing of traits occurs. Instead of being a melting pot, the theory goes, America is a collection of ethnic groups, each preserving its own culture but getting along reasonably well with others, politically and economically. The individual does not go it alone, isolated from countrymen and culture. This alternative to assimilation is called *cultural pluralism.*

Cultural pluralism became especially popular in the 1960s when Americans became interested in ethnicity and began looking for their roots. Michael Novak, a Slovak, wrote about it in a book aptly called *The Rise of the Unmeltable Ethnic.* Groups such as the blacks and the Catholic and Jewish immigrants of the 1920s valued their own heritage above the ideal of assimilation. There was a rise in ethnic consciousness and a realization that ethnicity could not be so easily shed.

To begin the acculturation process, the immigrant finds a job and a place to live, learns the language, and puts children in school. Joining the mainstream is easier for some than for others—easier for the young than for the old, easier for those who go out into the city or town than for those who stay home, easier for the well-educated professional, who is more easily accepted by Americans, than for those who came from the rural lower classes. The professional has more contact with the dominant culture and shares the middle-class goals of achievement and success. The lower-class immigrant may place more value on family loyalty than on economic achievement.

The early adjustment is also easier for the immigrant than for the refugee. Immigrants want to come to the United States; they have high hopes and ambition for themselves. They are determined and willing to take risks; otherwise they would not be immigrants.

Refugees, by contrast, are forced out of their homelands.

They do not choose to leave and may be quite sad and bitter about the move. They have a psychological adjustment to make to the new country that the immigrant does not. Refugees must realize that conditions will not change soon enough for them to be able to return to their homelands before they can begin to think positively about life in the United States.

Among recent immigrants, the Cuban exiles of the 1960s have made the transition from refugee to Cuban-American; the Vietnamese of the 1970s have not. Studies have shown that many Vietnamese refugees were experiencing psychosomatic respiratory and digestive illnesses even a year after they arrived. Many also felt inadequacy, anger, and tension.

Finding a good job is essential to the refugee's adjustment. It restores a sense of self-worth and provides contacts with other people, an opportunity to learn and use the language, and a way to discover and conform to American life. Refugees with a high occupational status may be forced to take menial jobs until they can learn the language and meet professional requirements. Some careers, such as those in medicine, plumbing, science, carpentry, and engineering, are more transferable internationally than others, such as those in law, creative writing, journalism, religion, politics, and popular music.

After three or four years, if the refugees have not adjusted, their determination and drive decrease and they begin to pin their hopes on their children. They may become bogged down in low-level jobs that offer a regular paycheck and a sense of security but no advancement or transition to the mainstream. Paradoxically, many of those who become angry at the refugee experience do better. They become more aggressive and resourceful and have a burning desire to make a place for themselves and to prove their worth.

One recent study of Portuguese immigrants shows that women play an important role in the family's adjustment. They are "the pushers, the naggers, the needlers, the schemers, the manipulators, the innovators, the security blankets, and the teachers." It is often the woman who pushes the family to immigrate. Caribbean women, in particular, seem independent enough to come on their own, work, and then send for their children. The woman's ability to manage the move and make contacts in the new community affects the family's sense of well-being. Whereas the male must find a job and get himself to work, the woman must learn the neighborhood, cope with social services, and know her way around.

The newest immigrants have had some advantages over the immigrants of seventy-five years ago. More private organizations and government agencies are willing to help them now, and the public is more aware of some of the problems immigrants face, particularly the psychological adjustment. Even so, English lessons, job training, access to welfare, and a sponsor do not reach the heart of the emotional adjustment. "You can't put a refugee in a camp for a few months, or even a couple of years, and then expect him to join the American mainstream. That's ridiculous!" one psychiatrist-researcher said. Pressures on the immigrant continue long after resettlement.

An individual immigrant is considered assimilated, according to the sociologist Robert E. Park, "as soon as he has shown that he can get on in the country." He or she has a suitable job, speaks English easily, lives in uncrowded conditions, has children who are succeeding in school, and has sufficient social contact with others. He or she has also decided to stay in the United States and become a citizen. (The number of applications for citizenship went up 68 percent from

1971 to 1979, paralleling the increase in immigration.) Some less quantifiable indicators of assimilation are a color TV set, a selection of the latest popular records, a preference for hamburgers and french fries, and fluent use of American slang.

As individuals are assimilated, what happens to the group? American culture stresses self-help, relying on oneself rather than on family or community. To succeed, a newcomer may have to subordinate family, neighborhood, and community to career. To enter the mainstream, the immigrant, too, must adopt the behavior and attitudes of the dominant culture. But such assimilation can move too fast. Immigrants may become demoralized and fail to be proud of their culture and heritage and pass it on to their descendants. One writer says that the immigrant has had "to learn loneliness" in order to become Americanized. The United States is the only immigrant-receiving country that does not encourage immigrants to make the adjustment as a group.

Immigrant groups have traditionally provided warmth, familiar ways, and a sense of acceptance that softens the uprooting that has taken place. Somewhat protected from the larger society, individuals can adjust at their own pace. At first, the group offers merely people to talk to, people who speak the same language. It may also offer tips about jobs, information on how to get a bus downtown or apply for a Social Security card, occasional baby-sitting and supervision of children, and people with whom to share a holiday.

On a broader scale, groups offer recreational and religious activities. The Pan-American Soccer League, for example, is a U. S. organization made up of soccer clubs whose members are of various Latin American nationalities. Many Hispanic and West Indian soccer and cricket teams play in the parks of New York City .

The Catholic church has long been the church of the immigrant—first of the Irish and Germans, later of the southern and eastern Europeans, and now of the French-Canadians, Mexicans, Puerto Ricans, and some West Indians. The "ethnic church" has had a significant part in keeping the ethnic community together. The church has not played as active a role as many would urge, however, in helping groups such as Mexican-Americans with educational, legal, and economic problems. Also, its hierarchy lags behind the ethnic makeup of its parishes. In the early 1970s, for example, the Irish constituted only one-fifth of the Catholics in the United States but about one-third of the clergy and one-half the hierarchy.

The mass celebration of holidays is another function of the group. The Vietnamese in Iowa get together to celebrate their New Year. West Indians have an annual parade in Brooklyn. Colombians meet annually in Flushing Meadow Park in Queens.

The community can be protective at first but provide paths into the mainstream as the immigrant becomes more acclimated. It can be particularly helpful to the old, who may never venture beyond it, but somewhat stifling to the young, who may see it as too restrictive and narrow-minded. The group helps individuals avoid welfare, it helps them deal with physical or mental illness, and it helps prevent school dropouts and delinquency.

Each nationality varies in its adjustment. One problem for the Indo-Chinese, according to Dr. William Liu of the Asian-American Mental Health Research Center in Chicago, has been that their character tended to be more passive than that of U. S. natives. Hispanic women, too, have trouble being assertive. They have been taught to accept authority, to conform in behavior, and to fear the outside world. Some groups suffer more from racial discrimination than others.

The assimilation-acculturation process is a long one.

Only the second or third generations finally feel comfortable in the United States and recoup some of the status the first generation lost. As the second generation matures, some conflict with the immigrant parents is almost inevitable. The child adopts many American values that are at odds with ethnic values. When children are used as interpreters and guides for the parents, the parents' authority is further undermined. Immigrant parents lose authority at the very moment they feel it is most important to protect the child from the problems of American youth.

Most of the newest immigrants—those who have come since 1965—have not been here long enough to have made the long-term adjustment. But the pace of adaptation and participation has seemed more rapid. Many of the newest immigrants do not settle in an urban ethnic neighborhood to begin with but move straight to outlying neighborhoods or suburbs. The overall pattern of immigrant settlement has changed, too. INS statistics for 1979 show that most aliens live in California, Texas, New York, and Florida. But New York is no longer the funnel for immigrants it used to be. In 1940 one in every four aliens lived in New York; in 1979 only one in fifteen did. California now has one in four.

One indication of group acculturation is involvement in politics. Let us look briefly at the extent to which recent Asians, Hispanics, Caribbeans, and others have entered American politics.

Politics

The first generation of immigrants usually has little interest in American politics and little political impact. If they are involved at all it is in the politics of the country they left.

Cubans, Iranians, Russian dissidents, Serbo-Croatians, Armenians, Chileans, and some Puerto Ricans have demanded attention for their native causes, sometimes with demonstrations, bombings, and even assassinations. Very small groups of terrorists are responsible for the violence, but they may be the extreme expression of the views of the majority.

The longer aliens remain here, the less hope they have of bringing about change at home. Cuban extremists began using terrorist tactics when their anti-Castro cause looked increasingly hopeless. Similarly, Serbian and Croatian émigrés became more desperate in their actions when relations improved between Yugoslavia and the United States. Once immigrants have been here twenty or thirty years, their children have grown, many have become citizens, and they begin to register, vote, and organize.

Hispanics and Asians have yet to become strong political forces in the United States, although Chicanos in the Southwest have begun to organize. Some West Indians have been political leaders, but they have been only moderately successful in promoting the cause of the black minority. Europeans—Poles, Irish, Italians—invented ethnic politics but recent arrivals do not necessarily fit the established patterns.

Mexican-Americans provide an example of how immigrants eventually enter politics. Those more established in the United States have been described as an emerging "brown middle America." Their political emergence has been slow. Although a few organizations existed before the 1960s, the first major Mexican-American political movement grew out of the farm workers' strike. Its leader, Cesar Chavez, became a Mexican-American hero and inspired the Chicano political movement.

The main Chicano organization to emerge from the heightened ethnic politics of the 1960s was La Raza Unida, which was organized as a regional party in south Texas in 1970. José Angel Gutierrez founded LRU to capture control of his hometown. Crystal City had a population of 8,000 that was almost completely Mexican-American. Within two years, LRU controlled Crystal City, held much power in the county government, and had developed a statewide organization. It gained 6 percent of the vote in the 1972 gubernatorial election but was later beset by divisions and factionalism. Among LRU's demands were comprehensive, well-funded educational and economic programs for Mexican-Americans, who make up one-fifth of the population in Texas.

Mexican-Americans have potential political strength in many cities in the Southwest, but their numbers have only recently been reflected in elected positions. In San Antonio, for example, they constitute 50 percent of the population; enough are citizens to elect four of the eleven city council members. New Mexico, where one-third of the population speaks Spanish, usually has one Hispanic senator and one Anglo. The governor and lieutenant governor alternate in ethnic identity. In Denver, Mexican-Americans make up 13 percent of the population but until recently had no voice on the thirteen-member city council. Both Houston and Dallas were forced to change their methods of electing city council members to assure some minority representation.

Los Angeles is becoming a Hispanic city. About 28 percent of the general population and almost 50 percent of the school population is Hispanic, mostly Mexican. "A few years ago, the Latins didn't recognize their power and were almost embarrassed if they were victimized," a police officer commented. "But all of a sudden, they're coming into their own, feeling their strength and starting to assert themselves politically." Native whites are in the minority in Los Angeles, with

44 percent of the population. Blacks, Hispanics, and Asians together form a majority.

National politicians have begun to court the Mexican-American vote. Mexican-Americans usually vote Democratic, and they were enthusiastic supporters of John Kennedy in 1960. But in 1972 President Nixon fashioned a "Chicano strategy." He spent $47 million in federal money on projects for Spanish-speaking citizens and appointed Hispanics to his administration. As a result, he received 31 percent of the Spanish-speaking vote when he ran for re-election, according to a CBS analysis. Since Mexican-Americans now represent up to one-third of the total electoral vote in California, New Mexico, Colorado, and Texas, future candidates will continue to woo them.

Political participation comes more naturally for the newest immigrants if a preceding generation has established the place of the ethnic group in American society. Mexican-Americans and Europeans have this advantage. Asians, who were not allowed to immigrate in large numbers before 1965, except to Hawaii, do not. Hiram L. Fong and Daniel K. Inouye were the first Asian-Americans elected to Congress, both in 1959, followed by Spark M. Matsunaga in 1962 and Patsy Mink in 1964.

Filipinos and Chinese both became more active during the ethnic surge of the 1960s, forming groups such as the Filipino-American Political Association and the Asian-American Political Alliance to work on human rights issues and to help their fellow ethnics. They gain more recognition in cities in the West, such as Los Angeles and Seattle, which have long been the main U. S. links with Asia and the choice of residence of many Asian immigrants.

Historically, immigrants have tended to be politically

conservative, supporting the free enterprise system. They have a strong belief in individualism, that those who are free to seek opportunity can be successful. The second generation, however, often turns toward liberalism, partly as a reaction to the "old-fashionedness" of the first generation. Thus, Asian and Mexican-American activists stress the human rights of their people and attack discrimination.

As immigrants become more active politically, they come into conflict with the sons and daughters of other immigrants and with other minorities. Chicanos and Vietnamese came to blows on Denver's west side over public housing. In Los Angeles, as Mexican-Americans become more assertive, blacks become more resentful. Mexican-Americans have begun moving into and around Watts, displacing blacks from housing and competing for jobs and a greater share of public aid for minorities. Blacks particularly resent the illegal immigrants. "They move twenty or thirty people into one house, heap old jalopies outside and don't speak English," an unemployed black factory worker said. "The black people had to work and march to get where they are; these Mexicans come in illegally and take jobs. Is that fair?"

Sometimes conflicts arise between old and new immigrants of the same ethnic group. Second- and third-generation Chinese-Americans are scornful of those "fresh off the boat." And middle-class Mexican-Americans do not welcome competition from illegal Mexican immigrants.

Some of the conflict between ethnic groups was brought out by the 1980 census. Many groups, especially Hispanics, feared they would not be fully counted. An undercount means less representation in Congress and less federal money, when it is distributed according to population. Community workers stressed that a full count would bring local communities more health clinics, job training, housing, day-care centers, playgrounds, bilingual education, and similar services. As in the past, numbers mean power, a lesson the newest immigrants will learn quickly.

The Uncommitted Commuter

Once immigrants start voting, organizing political parties, bringing lawsuits to counter discrimination, being counted in the census, paying income taxes, and going to PTA meetings, they have committed themselves to the American way. There are many, however, who have not decided to stay. Modern transportation and communication make it easier for immigrants to cling to their homelands, geographically and psychologically. Home, for some, is several hundred dollars and three to five hours away.

More immigrants today come to try out life here, to make money, to return if they don't like it, and perhaps to come back again. A recent study by the Mexican government found that most illegal Mexican migrants cross the border with the intention of returning in just a few months. Mexicans are not the only ones who "commute," however. In the Western Hemisphere, in particular, Caribbean peoples and Latin Americans return frequently to their native countries for vacations or holiday seasons, when a relative becomes ill or dies, or when their visa numbers come up.

Many feel they are between two cultures. They can easily compare the new environment with the old. Some aspects of American life compare unfavorably: the pace of life, discrimination, the poor treatment of old people, the divorce rate and geographical separation of the extended family, the crime rate, and drug abuse. America is often seen as a good place to make money but not the best place to live, especially when compared with a tropical island. "We don't work [at home] like we do here," was a frequent comment from different immigrants.

Commuting reinforces cultural pluralism; assimilation no longer seems possible or even desirable. More of today's immigrants resist giving up their own culture. Hispanics cling to their language, Indians to their religion.

Bilingualism

Clinging to the native language is a crucial aspect of preserving culture. The old immigrants were expected to give up their native languages. Polish or Swedish might be spoken at home or in church, but English was to be used in school and at work. German was a much-used language at the turn of the century, until the United States entered World War I against Germany. If an ethnic group wanted to maintain its language, it sponsored native-language schools—Hebrew schools, Greek schools—to be attended after American school.

Bilingualism has become more common, more accepted, and more valued today, especially among Hispanics. Census data from 1975 showed that Spanish was the second most widely used language after English. It is spoken by 2.5 percent of the population. (The next most common are Chinese, spoken by 0.2 percent, and Filipino, spoken by 0.1 percent.) Unlike previous immigrant waves, in which immigrants spoke many different languages, Spanish is a predominant language among the newest immigrants.

The prevalence of Spanish has led to bilingualism in education, advertising, elections, and public service publications. The New York City Board of Education first provided bilingual education citywide in 1974. In California, Pacific Telephone is introducing a Spanish-language supplement to its telephone directories. In Chicago, the notices on buses and trains are posted in Spanish and English. Philadelphia offers its civil service exams and prints school report cards in both languages. Yet the working language remains English, and most Hispanics admit the necessity of speaking English if one wants to get ahead.

But continuing to speak Spanish is not only a matter of pride in Hispanic identity. "To me it would be a disgrace if they couldn't speak Spanish," Fernando Martinez said of his sons. "I feel it is important to learn perfectly another language just for the sake of knowing another language."

Bilingual education is a controversial subject. The federal government has supported it, and 80 percent of Hispanics favor it, but many Americans see it as catering to the Spanish-speaking in a way that was never done for previous immigrants. Bilingual education is an especially sensitive subject in Florida, which has many elderly residents who are first- or second-generation immigrants and had to learn English quickly. In a bilingual city like Miami both blacks and whites are at a disadvantage when job hunting if they can't speak Spanish.

Hispanics favor bilingual education for two reasons: they believe it will help their children learn, and they want to maintain the language. "If we lose the tradition of speaking Spanish, we lose our culture," said a twenty-seven-year-old Puerto Rican. "It is the soul of the people. Past migrations lost their languages, and this caused them much emotional damage. Our culture is very strong, and we will not lose what is ours."

Yet Americans fear the establishment of a second official

language. Resentment is based on the belief that "to be an American, you have to speak English" or that because non-Hispanics didn't have bilingual education, Hispanics shouldn't either. "The hidden issue in bilingual education," says David Lopez, executive director of the Puerto Rican Association for Community Action in New York, "is the perception that Americans feel all must speak English as a melting pot theory."

One of the strongest arguments for bilingual education has been the high drop-out rate among Hispanic children. Of every one hundred Puerto Rican students who enter high school in New York City, only about thirty graduate. The city-wide drop-out rate for Hispanics in Los Angeles was estimated at 68 percent in 1977. "If our schools were hospitals, and 50 percent of the patients didn't make it, the city would be up in arms," said a woman advocating more parent involvement in the schools. Those of Spanish origin complete a median 10.4 years of school, as compared with 11.3 for blacks and 12.3 for the total population.

In addition to maintaining ethnic identity and furthering academic education, proficiency in two languages is an advantage in a cosmopolitan world. Nine out of ten Americans cannot speak, read, or effectively understand any language but English. Education that leads to a high degree of bilingualism in English and a minority language would be an asset to the country.

This chapter has been concerned with the economic and political impact of immigrants and the process of acculturation. As seen in the discussion of bilingual education, Americans' reactions to the immigrants inevitably affects the acculturation experience. In many ways, Americans seem less threatened by immigrants today. They fear economic competition less and appreciate diversity more, an apprecition nurtured by generations of immigrants.

But in the last quarter of the twentieth century, there is also a feeling of uncertainty about immigrants and concern that immigrants not exacerbate racial problems. There is still a fear of large numbers of foreigners, an awareness of the poverty that already exists in the country, and a belief that we should look after our own first. That immigrants generally succeed economically and enrich our culture with their diversity is unquestioned, but the painfulness of the process and its potential for increasing ethnic conflict is also apparent. All these considerations are necessary parts of the assessment of U. S. immigration policy, the topic of the next two chapters.

Chapter VII
ILLEGAL IMMIGRATION

If we could count them, we could catch them.

IMMIGRATION TO the United States proceeds on two levels: legal and illegal. Two versions of reality exist in immigration policy: the first is what the law says, what Congress intended, and what INS tries to enforce, and the second is what actually happens. This disparity is the main problem with present U. S. policy. Twice as many immigrants come outside the provisions of the law each year as come legally.

Numbers

No one knows how many illegal aliens there actually are in the United States. A former INS commissioner, Leonard Chapman, summed up the difficulty: "If we could count them, we could catch them." Estimates in the 1970s ranged up to 12 million, but recent studies indicate far fewer. The Census Bureau estimated fewer than 6 million in 1980 and possi-

147

bly only 3.5 to 5 million. INS figures seem to indicate an upswing. The service apprehended more than a million illegal aliens each year in 1977, 1978, and 1979, compared with some 20,000 annually in the early 1960s. The number apprehended is not an accurate count of illegal aliens who actually come, however, because one alien may be apprehended several times, even in one night.

Whatever the real figures, Americans think that large numbers of illegal immigrants are coming here, especially from Mexico, the Caribbean islands, and Central America. The reasons for the increase are several. Visas from Western Hemisphere countries have been harder to obtain since 1965 and a long wait is required in many countries. Low air fares make it easier to come on a tourist visa and overstay. Improving economies in the sending countries also enable immigrants to earn enough money to leave. "Right now [1978] the price of a ticket is a year's wages for some people in Haiti and elsewhere," said a former commissioner, Lionel Castillo, "but as more and more people earn better wages, they will be trying to get to the United States."

The two types of illegal immigrants are EWIs (entry without inspection) and visa abusers. EWIs come in without obtaining the authorized documents to immigrate. Visa abusers enter with a legal visa but overstay it or violate its terms, by taking a job, for example. Visa abusers represent only about 12 percent of the illegal aliens apprehended.

Aliens can enter the country illegally without inspection in several ways. A Mexican who swims across the Rio Grande to Texas to evade customs inspectors will arrive wet—*mojado*—hence the terms "wet" and "wetback" to refer to illegal entrants. Some travel by boat to Puerto Rico or the Virgin Islands, obtain false U. S. birth or baptismal certificates, and then fly to the mainland. Others fly to Toronto and Montreal and find smugglers who will drive them over the border at night, using uninspected back roads. Illegal aliens often follow legal immigrants and settle where they can fade into an established ethnic community.

The Migration Stream

Two writers studied how one extended Dominican family—the Dominguez family—gradually immigrated to New York over a period of thirteen years, from 1962 to 1975. (Vivian Garrison and Carol I. Weiss, "Dominican Family Networks and United States Immigration Policy: A Case Study," *International Migration Review,* Summer 1979, 13:2.) Their story shows the many ways a would-be immigrant can come to the United States both legally and illegally. It also shows how a family that is determined to remain together must use and sometimes circumvent U. S. immigration law.

The Dominguez family in 1962 consisted of Papa and Mama, six daughters, and two sons. Three daughters were married and living outside the family home. The rest of the family lived together in one household. Papa's sister had married an American twenty years before and had moved to Florida. She provided the first U. S. connection.

The immigration stream began when the husband of Maria, a married daughter, was killed in an accident on his job. Maria moved to the United States to help take care of a cousin's household and two-year-old child. Her immigration was legal. She had secured working papers certifying that she was needed to fill that job before she left the Dominican Republic. She is described by her family as "the one who came best."

The husband of another daughter, Rosa, soon died of

natural causes, leaving her with two children to support in a country where the jobs available to women pay very little. In order to help Rosa immigrate, the family arranged a "marriage for favor." In the United States Maria had met a man who was a permanent resident alien; he was "legal." They planned to marry, but she asked him to marry her sister first so Rosa could come to the United States under the preference category for spouses of permanent residents. He did.

Meanwhile Papa had a heart attack and had to retire. The family's financial status declined. Raul, the oldest son, came to New York on a tourist visa and overstayed. Rosa had become a permanent resident by then and "asked for" both her children and her parents, under preference categories for relatives. Papa and Mama came in 1971.

Over the next several years, Papa and Mama brought other members of the extended family: a grandchild, whom they brought in as their son; their youngest son Pedro, who overstayed a tourist visa; a grandchild with "borrowed" papers that showed him to be a great-grandchild born a U. S. citizen while his mother was visiting; and their youngest daughter Luz, who "came the worst."

Luz's husband had come to the United States on a tourist visa, found a good job, and stayed on illegally. In order to bring Luz and their two children he divorced her and arranged a "marriage for business" to a legal resident. It cost him $700 but legalized his status. Then he could divorce again, remarry Luz, and bring his family in legally. Papa became impatient at the long process, however. For $1,200 he bought a passport with a tourist visa that could be used for a one-way trip and then returned to the seller. Luz used the passport to join her former husband but could not bring her children right away.

Thus through convoluted and complicated means, a migration chain was established. Seven of the adult members of the Dominguez family and four of their children immigrated to the United States. Luz's two children will come eventually, and at least seven more Dominguez children have been born here. Three grown daughters remain in the Dominican Republic with two children, supported by Papa's pension from the Dominican Republic, the rental of the family house, and money from the United States. Despite long separations and "paper" marriages, the Dominguez family managed to relocate together and improve their economic status.

The story of the Dominguez family illustrates how legal immigration and illegal immigration are intertwined and how a family determined to preserve its own values can use the preferences the law gives to spouses and children to its own advantage. Their immigration reveals, too, how a visitor, once here, can obtain legal status as a permanent resident alien and thus circumvent the intent of the preference system.

Economic Impact

Besides family reunification, the initial and recurring attraction of immigration for the Dominguez family was the same as for others: economic. Earlier illegal immigrants came mostly to work in agriculture, but since the 1960s, farms have become more mechanized. The majority now go to large cities where the pay is higher, the chances of being found are smaller, and low-level jobs are available. Illegal aliens from the Caribbean and Latin America gravitate to the Hispanic and black communities in New York City. Poles come in through Canada to join friends and relatives in Chicago and Detroit. Mexicans and Central Americans go to West Coast cities. And Washington, D. C., attracts a mixture of Latins, Nigerians, Koreans, Ethiopians, and Iraqis, among others.

Whereas undocumented workers in agriculture often stay only temporarily, urban illegal aliens tend to be better educated, more skilled, and more likely to stay permanently.

The fact that illegals come here looking for jobs is the most controversial aspect of their presence. The popular belief is that illegal aliens take jobs away from native workers, depress wages and working conditions, and use social services excessively.

Let us consider each claim separately. First, illegals take jobs away from natives. Former Secretary of Labor Ray Marshall claimed in 1979 that the unemployment rate could be reduced from 6 to 3.7 percent by removing illegal aliens from the job market.

The counterargument employers make is that there are some jobs no American is willing to do. The owner of a seafood plant in Texas that employs illegal aliens says, "I would rather have American citizens working for me, but oyster opening is something people don't want to get into." Opening oysters is a tedious task, "day in, day out, in wet, damp, humid conditions," that may pay "a good shucker" seven dollars an hour. A restaurant entrepreneur in the same state says, "In our industries we get the immigrant [he hires Mexicans, many illegal] mainly because he's the only guy reporting to work. . . ." A dishwasher there earns two dollars an hour.

Experts agree there are jobs Americans won't take—the menial, unstable, dead-end jobs such as stitching a dress together or picking tomatoes for three dollars an hour. Employers see a growing reluctance by black workers to take low-level jobs. There is no longer a first generation of black migrants newly arrived in the cities from the South who will work at anything. Instead, blacks of the second generation reject jobs with low social status and look for job security or career advancement. A constant supply of new migrants is needed to fill the lowest jobs. It is thus an exaggeration to say that each illegal alien who works here takes a job away from an American.

The opposite view to taking jobs away is the one espoused by Michael Piore, an economist at the Massachusetts Institute of Technology. He says illegal aliens come here because jobs are available; the availability of low-paying jobs causes the flow of immigrants. The United States demands and benefits from cheap labor, a demographer says: "We benefit from it when we eat vegetables . . . , when we go to restaurants, when we go to hospitals, and in many other areas." Aliens are generally welcomed in times of prosperity and regarded as a threat only during a recession.

Excluding illegals might not make jobs available to natives for three other reasons. First, jobs held by illegal immigrants would disappear because of mechanization or automation. Second, jobs would follow the workers. Large companies would relocate in countries where labor is cheap. Zenith, Motorola, Memorex, Burroughs, and North American Rockwell, for example, have already opened plants in Mexico. And third, some marginal enterprises would go out of business because they can compete only if they pay low wages.

Keeping illegals out would not create the large number of jobs hoped for, and so we must question the validity of the first claim. There is more truth to the second claim, however, the claim that illegal aliens depress wages and working conditions. Employers who hire illegal entrants have several advantages. They don't have to pay fringe benefits like health insurance, overtime, pensions, vacations, or sick pay; they may ignore health and safety precautions; and their work force is flexible: they can fire workers at will. They can pay them "off the books," which means not keeping the records the government requires and not withholding income taxes and paying Social Security taxes or unemployment compensation. All transactions are in cash, and there is no record of the employment.

Illegal aliens are also perceived as hardworking and more passive than natives. "These immigrants come here, they work very hard, and we're pleased with them," one employer said. Employers responding to a *Los Angeles Times* survey said they preferred Mexican labor not only because it was cheap but because "Mexicans work harder." Because illegal aliens are afraid of being deported, they don't complain to the authorities, and they are therefore subject to exploitation.

The Labor Department looked for exploitation of workers recently in garment, construction, hotel and restaurant work in the large cities. Investigators found 1,600 employers who had underpaid their workers—many of them illegal aliens—by nearly $5 million. Most of the violations of wage and hour laws were in uncompensated overtime. "There are Americans who would work at these jobs for $2.90 an hour," a Labor Department official commented, "but they won't do it for a dollar and a half, or if they have to work sixteen hours a day."

Such exploitation is also the target of unions because underpaid workers provide unfair competition for their members and their members' employers. Unions have begun organizing aliens, arguing that it is no more illegal for union leaders to organize them than it is for employers to employ them. The International Ladies' Garment Workers' Union has begun a drive in the garment industry in California. More than 80 percent of the 100,000 workers there are Hispanic, and most have entered illegally. The California Division of

Labor Enforcement found that 999 of 1,083 manufacturers in the garment industry were violating state minimum wage and overtime laws. The union has recruited only about 10,000 members so far but says that illegal aliens have begun to assert themselves as they become used to a higher standard of living.

One problem with both enforcement of labor laws and unionization is that illegal aliens do not always see themselves as exploited. "What we might define as exploitation," says writer Austin T. Fragomen, "many illegals regard as the greatest opportunities of their lives. . . . They are basically law-abiding people trying to climb out of poverty and, in the truest sense of the American dream, they are willing to work for it."

The third claim—that illegals are a drain on social services—is generally unfounded, at least at first. The most common illegal immigrants are unmarried males and married men who come here without their families. A large number return home after having made enough money to improve their lives. They may affect the labor market and send a significant amount of money home, but they use few social services. They may also have paid income and Social Security taxes whose benefits they seldom receive.

When single men stay here and marry and when married men send for their families, they begin to settle here permanently. In this semi-permanent status they are more likely to use social services. They begin to send children to school, have babies delivered at the local hospital, and use more fire and police protection. INS often quotes $13 billion as the national annual cost in services to illegal aliens. (Other estimates start at $1 billion.)

Illegal immigrants' families use medical services and education most heavily. They are seldom covered by health insurance at work, and they're not eligible for Medicaid, government medical insurance for the poor. In an emergency, they depend on local public hospitals and often they cannot pay the high bills. A small county hospital in Merced, California, treated an illegal alien who had been critically injured in an auto accident. The county ended up paying approximately $76,000 for his medical care, almost its entire medical budget for the year. The care and treatment of illegal immigrants in Los Angeles County Hospital exceeded $8 million in 1974, a sum it tried to recoup from the federal government.

Los Angeles County estimated that it also spent at least $150 million in 1975 educating the children of illegal aliens. The education issue has come to the fore in Texas, where the legislature passed a law in 1975 saying illegal aliens were not entitled to free public education. The state argued that it cannot afford to educate an estimated 100,000 more children and provide the necessary bilingual and compensatory programs.

"Since the federal government isn't enforcing the immigration laws and they're not going to give us the money to pay for it, we decided we're going to educate only our own students," Susan Dasher, an assistant state attorney general, said. A federal district court judge found the law unconstitutional in April 1980, but some school districts continued to seek legal relief from the obligation.

Critics of the law point out that the state is unwilling to spend much money on education to begin with. Texas has no state or local income taxes and ranks about fortieth in the country in the amount it spends for education. Critics look at the long-term effect, too. "These are future Americans," says Thomas P. Carter, an education professor in California's state university system. "These are not future Mexicans, and they perceive themselves as discriminated against by Americans." They will be uneducated, too.

The claim that large numbers of illegal entrants receive welfare is largely false. To obtain a Social Security card or to receive welfare, food stamps, Medicaid, or unemployment compensation, one must be a citizen. Sometimes the eligibility screening is not effective, but by and large only the American-born children of illegal aliens receive benefits. One of the most reliable studies (done by David North and M. P. Houston for the Department of Labor in 1976) showed that three-fourths of the illegal immigrants surveyed had income taxes and Social Security taxes withheld from their wages. Only half of 1 percent were on welfare; 1½ percent received food stamps; 4 percent got unemployment compensation; and 4½ percent had taken advantage of public health and medical programs.

When local and state governments complain about the burden of illegal immigrants, they reveal a problem in immigration policy. The policy is made at the national level, but financial effects are felt at the local level. When national policy winks at illegal immigrants, it reflects an ambiguity in the public attitude. On the local level, Americans fear job competition, the lowering of wages and their standard of living. In the abstract, we recognize the advantage of a cheap labor supply and are sympathetic to those who are willing to work hard to support their families. We have so far been unwilling to do what would be necessary to keep them out.

Ironically the American government has been put in the position of defending the rights of illegal aliens. When illegal Salvadoreans died in the Arizona desert, the smugglers were prosecuted. When two Arizona brothers beat and robbed three Mexicans who walked across their land, the Justice Department brought charges. The U. S. Department of Labor forces employees to pay even undocumented workers the minimum wage and overtime.

What has been developing within the last ten years, however, is an underground community of people who live outside the law and avoid any contact with government. They are subject to exploitation by employers and by immigration lawyers and "consultants" who make promises they do not have to keep. They are preyed upon by criminals because they are reluctant to report a crime. They represent a potential health hazard when unwilling to seek treatment or immunization. "It can't be in the best interests of this country to have a whole population of people who are without rights, people who can't vote, people who have to live in constant fear of detection," said Dr. Vernon Briggs, a labor economist at Cornell University. "It's becoming a problem we can't ignore any longer even if we want to."

The Select Commission described the problem as a breakdown in both law and policy. We select some immigrants with great care but allow twice as many others to come in the back door. The basic problem is one of control. The attractions for the illegal immigrant are stronger than the enforcement measures. If the United States can decide how many immigrants to admit and who they should be, can the resulting immigrant flow be controlled? This question underlies all other issues in immigration policy.

Chapter VIII
PROBLEMS AND POLICY

The overriding issue . . . is sheer numbers.

UNITED STATES immigration policy is believed by many to be out of control. Few people have understood the workings of the law since 1965, but they see and read what happens daily: Haitians arrive by the boatload on the Florida coast; Cubans storm the Peruvian embassy in Havana trying to emigrate to the United States; Salvadoreans die of thirst in the Arizona desert after being smuggled across the border. The United States reacts to each crisis with compassion, but the practical problems generate a response that is less generous.

Americans are particularly uneasy about illegal immigration. The columnist James Reston expressed that concern in the spring of 1980 as Cubans and Haitians were arriving in Florida: "The U. S. government has clearly lost control of its immigration policy. . . . Even at a time of high inflation and unemployment [this country] is not able to protect its borders or enforce its laws against the entry of illegal aliens."

159

The concern arises despite recent changes in immigration law. Since 1965 our policy has been more egalitarian, with no racial or ethnic quotas and no differential limits for countries. The result has been an ethnically diverse wave of immigrants who are more often Asian and Hispanic than European. The United States has also sought to reunite families separated by immigration, to welcome the skilled and educated, grant asylum to political refugees, encourage unskilled workers but protect American workers, and maintain some control over foreign visitors and students.

These principles have not been fully implemented because there is a gap between the theory of immigration law and the way that law works. Officially, only a certain number of immigrants may come each year, and they must fit one of the preference categories. Unofficially, the limits are only guidelines, and the categories can be manipulated. In practice we have an inconsistent immigration policy.

Hypothetical case 1: A nurse in the Philippines does not pass the pre-board exam given there and cannot obtain a visa as a needed professional. But because she has a sister here, she immigrates instead as a relative of a permanent resident alien.

Hypothetical case 2: A worker from Jamaica waits patiently for the labor certification he needs to immigrate legally. Meanwhile, his friend obtains a tourist visa, finds a job in the United States, overstays his visa, and with the help of a lawyer begins adjusting his status to that of a legal alien, all before his fellow worker in Jamaica ever receives his visa.

Hypothetical case 3: A Cuban exile who comes on a boat from Mariel in the spring of 1980 is automatically granted political asylum, even though she admits that her main reason for coming was economic. A Haitian arrives after June 1980 and also asks for asylum, although she is actually fleeing starvation. But she is deported because she has not been able to prove a well-founded fear of persecution.

Thus, having relatives in this country, understanding immigration law, and knowing how U. S. foreign policy regards one's native country become the important practical considerations in whether or not a person can immigrate to the United States. In one recent year, only 6 percent of the legal immigrants came in without being related to someone already here. The competition for visas in some Western Hemisphere countries has spurred illegal immigration.

Much of the gap between law and reality comes in enforcement. As demonstrated by the effort to locate Iranian students and by the large number of undocumented Mexicans who succeed in crossing the border each day, the Immigration and Naturalization Service is overburdened. It cannot enforce the laws except on a selective basis.

When refugees are concerned, the United States seems increasingly forced to react to each world crisis as it occurrs.

Underlying these problems is public ambivalence about immigration. Americans value the economic and cultural contributions immigrants make to American life. But there is also a growing awareness of the need to be more attentive to minorities already here. Americans have traditionally welcomed diversity, but there is unease when non-Anglos become predominant in a city such as Los Angeles or Miami. There is concern about maintaining a high standard of living in the face of overpopulation and dwindling resources.

IN RESPONSE to this unease and to the charges that immigration law is out of date, Congress established the Select Commission on Immigration and Refugee Policy in 1978. The commission's task was to conduct a thorough study of immigration law and practice and recommend a new policy. The study necessarily involved three basic questions:

1. How many immigrants should the United States accept?
2. Whom should it welcome?
3. How can the government control immigration?

Let us consider answers to these questions in terms of what U. S. immigration policy should be.

How Many?

Two opposing phrases—"open door" and "the good life"—are often repeated when legislators argue about how many immigrants to admit. An open door is the Statue of Liberty image of what U. S. immigration policy should be: accept anyone who seeks freedom and has the gumption to get here. The open door has been largely a myth, however, at least in the twentieth century. There have been restrictions, both quantitative and qualitative, on who may come. In 1924 the annual ceiling was 150,000; in 1980 it was 270,000. The Select Commission recommended a 350,000 yearly limit.

But compared with other countries, the United States has had a relatively open door. The modern debate centers on whether to leave it open. An ecologist and conservationist who testified at Select Commission hearings invoked both phrases. "An open-door immigration policy by the United States can do very little toward ameliorating the world population problem of overcrowding and famine," Dr. M. King Hubbert said, "but it has the potentiality of destroying what remains of the good life in the United States."

Dr. Hubbert's views are shared by those who want to

maintain the good life by controlling population growth, preserving resources, and protecting jobs. The population of the
United States is now 222.5 million and will reach at least 250
million by the year 2000. With the current fertility rate of 1.8
children per woman, zero population growth will not be
reached for another fifty or so years. If the effects of immigration are included, the population will increase by an additional 24 million by 2000. (This is projected at the current rate
of more than a million immigrants a year, 400,000 legal and
800,000 illegal.) Thus immigration will nearly double the
U. S. growth rate and postpone the attainment of zero population growth.

The immigration rate is unlikely to decline. Nine million
foreigners have applied to come here legally. Millions more
will come illegally if they can. "The overriding issue in immigration policy is not race, not ethnicity, not even job skills,"
says Roger Conner of the Federation for American Immigration Reform (FAIR). "It's sheer numbers." FAIR is an out-
growth of the zero-population-growth movement and op-
poses further large increases in immigration.

The greatest population pressures, of course, come from
outside the border. Many Third World populations are still
increasing at a rapid rate, and countries will try to ease
crowding by encouraging emigration. The populations of nations such as Kenya, Iraq, Mexico, Brazil, and Egypt will
more than double in the next twenty-six years. Although a
World Fertility Survey shows fertility and birthrates actually
declining, no early relief is in sight. The earth's population
will increase 50 percent by 1990 and reach 11 billion by the
third quarter of the twenty-first century, before the population explosion may perhaps stop.

Americans who are trying to make the world better for
their children by having fewer of them feel threatened by the
higher reproduction rates of some foreigners. Many immi-

grants use fewer contraceptive methods, place more value on large families, and see the birth of a child, who is automatically a U. S. citizen, as an aid to legalizing the parents.

Some of the fears are exaggerated, however. Most second-generation immigrants have about the same number of children as natives do. The Select Commission found that population growth in the United States is much more affected by slight changes in fertility rates than it is by immigration. Emigration, too, must be taken into account. As few as 37,000 or as many as 150,000 immigrants and citizens (depending on whose estimate is used) leave the country for good each year.

Along with the threat of overpopulation, we have experienced a growing awareness of the scarcity of resources. As a population grows, the demand for food increases, but the simultaneous urbanization of agricultural land reduces the capacity to produce food. Some experts predict that this country will have no food to export by the end of the century.

One response the United States could make is to set a target population size for the country and set immigration restrictions in line with the target. Advocates of zero population growth believe that the total number of immigrants should not exceed the total number of emigrants, with the exception of immediate families of citizens. Using the Census Bureau estimate of 37,000 emigrants a year, they would restrict legal immigration to about 40,000, one-tenth the number who come legally now.

Such a reduction would necessitate a radical change in immigration policy. Despite the arguments for increased restriction, such a change seems unlikely, given the persistence of the open-door image in the American mind. Underlying the conservationist view, too, is a premise that the good life should be preserved for those who already have it, but this is not an international view. The Select Commission recommended an increase to 350,000 in the annual ceiling with more control of illegal immigration.

Whom Shall We Welcome?

Whom shall we welcome is in some ways an easier question to answer. The United States has traditionally welcomed three types of people: those seeking freedom—political refugees; those seeking opportunity—economic immigrants; and those joining a close member of the family—spouses and children. Recently, the concepts of freedom, opportunity, and family have become harder to define and even harder to limit.

POLITICAL REFUGEES

Since 1945 the United States has admitted more than 1.8 million refugees: Europeans displaced by the German and Soviet troops during World War II, Hungarians fleeing the failed revolution of 1956, Hong Kong Chinese, Czechoslovakians, Cubans, Indo-Chinese, and Soviet Jews. But until 1980 the definition of a political refugee in U. S. immigration law was limited to those fleeing a communist country or those who had been displaced in the Middle East.

That narrow definition was obviously inadequate, as was the ceiling of 17,400 refugees a year. When pressures peaked in 1979, with large numbers of Soviet Jews and Indo-Chinese applying for admission, Congress broadened the definition. It now includes anyone "who cannot return to his own country because of a well-founded fear of persecution because of race, religion, nationality, political opinion." This definition conforms to the United Nations Convention Relating to the Status of Refugees and covers those fleeing right-wing dictatorships, too, such as Haitians, Chileans, or Filipinos.

The Refugee Act of 1980 was an attempt to make a coherent, consistent policy for the admission of refugees. It raised the limit on the number admited to 50,000 a year and provided for the President to consult with Congress if there were additional refugees "of special humanitarian concern to the United States" who should be admitted on an emergency basis. A target of 234,000 refugees was set for 1980, however, to include 168,000 Indo-Chinese, 39,000 Soviet Jews, and 16,000 Cubans.

Refugees were to be admitted after proving they met the new definition. They would be aided in the resettlement process and given conditional entry for two years, after which they could become permanent resident aliens and eventually apply for citizenship.

The new legislation was undermined, however, even before it took effect. More than 100,000 Cubans set sail for Florida in 1980 without any permission to enter as refugees. Once they were here, it was hard to deport them. The group situation was similar to that of an individual who stows away on a ship or rushes into an embassy and makes an emotional appeal for freedom. If the freedom-seeker receives enough media attention, Americans usually respond sympathetically. A congressman may introduce a private bill legalizing the person's status. But accepting the stowaway raises the question of fairness to others from the source country who are still waiting patiently for their visas. Accepting large groups who can navigate to our borders raises the question of fairness to other nationalities contained by the 20,000-per-country limits.

The Carter administration's solution was to act outside the Refugee Act by allowing Cubans and Haitians who had arrived before June 21, 1980, to stay for six months as "entrants" until Congress decided their permanent status. The administration said future refugees would have to meet the 1980 act's definition. The decision had a potentially wide impact pointed out by an INS official: "If they can stay, the whole hemisphere is eligible."

If nations find it difficult to cope with sudden influxes of refugees, local communities find it even more threatening. Local governments in Florida in particular complained they were "picking up the tab on what is a national problem." Unlike other immigrants, refugees are eligible by law for a variety of help: Medicaid, welfare, public service jobs under the CETA Act, day care, and English-language training. They are given more aid because they have a more difficult and sudden adjustment to make. The federal government has reimbursed private agencies about $300 per refugee, but total costs per refugee were averaging $1,600 to $2,200, and additional costs fell to local governments. The Carter administration agreed to provide full federal reimbursement of state and local governments for their costs in providing medical assistance, special education, and social services to the entrants for one year.

Aside from financial concerns, the domestic reaction to refugees varies. When a large number arrive and settle in one area, such as Dade County, considerable resentment may result. Anglos fear they will be outnumbered, that more waves of Cubans will turn Miami into a completely Hispanic city. Governor Bob Graham of Florida thought the feeling of resentment was more widespread: "We are in a period where the national sympathy for refugees is at a low point," he said.

Minorities, especially, are resentful of the "open heart, open arms, and open federal purse" approach to refugees. "We spend millions of dollars to help the refugees come to this country," said the Reverend Kenneth Acey of Fort Wayne, Indiana, "while we have people who need homes, people who need to be fed, and people who need jobs. Blacks are being pushed over to the sidelines."

Clearly the United States cannot accept all who claim to be political refugees. The sheer numbers of refugees in the world are overwhelming. In 1980 there were 16 million, including Cambodians, Somalis, Palestinians, and Afghans in Pakistan, to mention only a few. Increasingly refugees are becoming an international problem, as sudden political upheavals, famines, and natural disasters make the twentieth century an "age of refugees."

OPPORTUNITY-SEEKERS

Although many immigrants say they are coming in search of freedom, the predominant motivation is usually economic. They come seeking a chance to move up in the world, to share the good life. One Haitian said she came for a better life and went on to explain that "in Haiti you make small money." A Barbadian said, "There's a whole lot of opportunity here."

It is hard for a country with a free enterprise tradition to deny an immigrant's desire to make a better life. Yet, during the latter part of the twentieth century, the gap between the rich and poor countries is so wide that it is impossible to admit everyone who wants to give capitalism a try. "Once you say 'economic refugee,' you've got the whole world," said one U. S. planner. The United States must decide which opportunity seekers to admit.

Recent legal immigrants have often been the cream of the crop of their home countries—professionals, managers, and skilled workers—the Martina Navratilovas and Mikhail Baryshnikovs of the world. The irrepressible opportunity-seekers have been the undocumented and unskilled but hard and frugal workers, those willing to pick lettuce for three dollars an hour.

One approach to selection is to act purely out of self-interest. "I think we should have the right to choose, should we wish to, whatever balance of existing ethnic or racial or skilled characteristics there would be," said Senator Alan K. Simpson of Wyoming. A premise of this outlook is that the migration of talented people is a natural phenomenon—they go where they can do the most good—and the United States should not turn away the talented if they want to come, no matter what the effect on the sending country.

One proposal has been to choose immigrants according to a point system like the one Canada instituted in 1976. Points are awarded to a prospective immigrant on the basis of occupational suitability, age, personal suitability, ability to speak the language, relationship to a Canadian resident, and willingness to settle in a remote area of Canada. (Formerly one-fourth of all Canadian immigrants headed for Toronto.)

The argument against selecting the best is that robbing developing countries of their human capital and investments in education runs counter to our long-term self-interest. Why give foreign aid with one hand if we take it away with the other? A survey by a House committee in 1973 concluded that the United States should encourage foreign physicians to stay home, for example, and provide contraceptive services and information to the growing populations there. A 1976 medical education law virtually stopped foreign doctors from entering this country.

Certification by the Department of Labor has been used as a way of admitting only those nonprofessional workers who are really needed. To qualify in the sixth category of the preference system (for skilled or unskilled workers needed in the U. S. labor market) immigrants must obtain certification from the department that they are needed to fill particular jobs and will not displace native workers. The system has not been working well, however. By the time a visa is approved (as much as two years after it is requested), job market conditions may have changed. And once they are here the immigrants are really free to take any job, not necessarily the ones they were certified for. Many advocate an expanded temporary worker program as an alternative. The present H-2 program authorized only about 30,000 workers in 1979.

FAMILY MEMBERS

The third group of immigrants is made up of family members. For purposes of immigration the definition of "family" has emphasized the nuclear unit—spouses and young children first and then older parents. The 1965 amendments also granted preference to brother, sisters, and married sons and daughters. These two preferences opened up whole new areas of immigration. They created a self-perpetuating stream based on the need to reunite the family in its new location, the United States. Immigrants often relate that it was an aunt who began the process, a brother who continued it, and the last niece or nephew who will complete it.

Family reunification has overwhelmed other goals of U. S. immigration policy, and some rethinking of its purpose is necessary. Lawrence Fuchs, executive director of the Select Commission, pointed out that the brother-sister preference grows geometrically by its very nature: "It literally explodes, leading to such demands that it clogs the system and prevents other people from coming in who should have priority access." It also works inequitably between different countries. The small child of a Mexican mother or father working here might be kept out as long as eight years, while the relative of a German immigrant can enter immediately because of differing demands for visas in those countries. Right now

700,000 close relatives of U. S. citizens or permanent residents are waiting for visas in countries that have already reached their annual ceiling.

Another problem with family reunification is that different cultures have different concepts of the family. To some West Indians, for example, the brother-sister or father-daughter relationship is more stable and dependable than the husband-wife bond, and a woman will more easily leave her husband behind to join siblings in the United States. In Asian cultures, older parents are given a special importance. And the Hispanic family tends to be more extended, too.

The Select Commission recommended continuing to emphasize family reunification but giving preference only to spouses, minor children, and the unmarried brothers and sisters of adult citizens. It also voted to ease the requirements for grandparents of citizens and elderly parents of legal resident aliens.

There are a few other considerations as to whom we should welcome. Should homosexuals continue to be excluded? Should immediate neighbors, Mexicans and Canadians, have larger quotas because of close historical ties and common borders? Should countries with long waiting lists be given higher quotas? Should the United States be a haven for the wealthy, for those who have money to invest here?

Whereas Congress is concerned with the domestic implications of those who are welcome, the executive branch often considers foreign policy. If we want to buy Mexican oil, can we constantly complain about Mexican migrant workers? Can we embarrass Russia by encouraging dissidents and defectors and still pursue detente? Can we encourage Afghans to revolt and not accept them as refugees when a revolution fails?

One principle the Select Commission agreed on was that race should not be a consideration in immigrant selection. A major change it proposed was the creation of a new category of immigrants. This category would include what the commission calls "seed immigrants." Chairman Theodore Hesburgh explained its purpose: "While compassion dictates openness to refugees and the reunification of close relatives, our national economic and cultural development has always depended on an infusion of ambitious, vigorous, 'seed immigrants' with no previous ties to the United States."

Selecting the seed immigrants might be problematical. One suggestion is to use a point system like the one adopted by Canada. Commission members hoped that the third category would help lessen the number of illegal immigrants.

The question of who is welcome is inextricably linked to that of how many are welcome. Both considerations depend on control. If we can't control the number of immigrants who come, how can we hope to be selective?

CONTROLLING THE FLOW

Can the United States really control all those who come into the country? The job of enforcing the immigration law lies with the Immigration and Naturalization Service, whose members consider the task impossible. Employees describe their jobs as "most frustrating."

"It gets to a point where after awhile there's just no enforcement," one employee said. "An awful lot of officers just give up."

The gap between the law and its enforcement comes about when there is a restrictive law on the national level but a lack of personnel on the border and a border so long and permeable that it stops few people. Those who want to stop illegal immigration do not always realize the magnitude of the problem. "The farther one gets from the border," one writer suggests, "the more faith one finds in enforcement as the solution to the problem."

The INS is part of the Justice Department. Its main duties are checking documents as people come into the country, apprehending illegal immigrants along the borders and inside the country, helping aliens become citizens, and keeping records. Its duties are part social service and part police work, helping some people into the country and keeping others out.

In both areas, its performance is inadequate, because of the volume of work. In recent years INS has been apprehending a million illegal aliens a year, processing more than 270 million people who come over the borders for various reasons, keeping track of more than 400,000 legal immigrants each year, and naturalizing 150,000.

From 1960 to 1970 congressmen said INS "was steadily losing control of the illegal alien situation" by hiding or minimizing the extent of the problem. As alien arrest rates zoomed, INS made only modest budget and staff requests, which were usually slashed. This led over the years to an increasing sense of futility. "For every one we pick up, it seems like there are ten more coming into the city and a hundred more already here," said an INS investigator in Washington, D. C. Paperwork is also overwhelming. Files are lost and misplaced, letters and phones go unanswered.

In addition to the volume of work, low morale, and lack of funds, INS has problems of corruption. Employees have taken gifts and favors from employers of illegal aliens who seek exemptions from enforcement; green cards—obtaining one is the first step in becoming a citizen—have been sold for as much as $20,000.

Much of the corruption occurs in the U. S. consulates

abroad (which are not part of INS), where all visas are issued. Bribe-taking is not uncommon. In Haiti $500 is the usual fee for a visa; in Hong Kong the price goes as high as $2,000 to $3,000. Fraud has become worse, according to one official, "because more people want to come."

INS has responded to the overload with technological improvements. The service has fashioned new "counterfeit-proof, impostor-proof, and tamper-proof" alien cards to replace the old green cards. The new cards can be read by computer, which means their validity can be checked quickly against records in Washington, D. C. The card bears the alien's photograph, fingerprint, signature, and coded biographical data.

The Border Patrol also uses the latest detection equipment: helicopters, sensors planted in major foot trails, and "a little black box." When placed on an automobile trunk or hay pile on a truck, the box can detect the heartbeat of a person hidden inside.

Internal enforcement is the most difficult task of INS. Aliens use the openness, freedom, large size, and heterogeneous population of the United States to their advantage, to become almost invisible people. INS concentrates its investigative force in the three largest cities—New York, Los Angeles, and Chicago. Current INS policy concentrates on finding illegal aliens at places of employment. Agents act only on citizen complaints or specific leads and must have search warrants or court orders or know the names of the aliens they are looking for. They don't follow anonymous tips unless the source is willing to testify in court or documentary evidence is available.

Because of the limitations on internal enforcement, INS has concentrated increasingly on preventing illegal entries at airports, seaports, and land borders. Such border control now

Hispanic-American organizations fear they
n a discriminatory way. Employers say they
o the work of immigration officers. There are
ial control and invasions of privacy.
ss, some members of the Select Commission
e cards as necessary to curb illegal immigra-
ricn Civil Liberties Union says that if such
d they should be accompanied by a constitu-
ent that sets principles for the management of
ernment. A cardless system has been proposed
ve. The work authorization information would
computer that could give employers clearance
nts.

issue remains thorny: Can we really have an
f we place restrictions on those who want to
The weight of opinion currently remains on the

nd proposal—to establish a temporary-worker
rebirth of the bracero idea. Its proponents rea-
United States needs a cheap, temporary, flexible
d that immigrants who currently come illegally
to come legally, work a few months, and return
ay illegal immigrants follow such a pattern any-
e bracero program was officially ended in 1964,
already knew the ropes of working in the United
ntinued to come illegally.
S. I. Hayakawa of California has recently intro-
osal to allow at least 500,000 Mexicans to come
ght-months visas. Workers would deposit $250
exican government, find their own jobs in the
es, and receive their deposits back when they re-
exico. They would be guaranteed another visa the
ar if they wanted it. The advantages to this coun-

involves more than 40 percent of INS personnel, most in the Border Patrol. The largest proportion of this force—85 percent—is placed on the 2,000-mile Mexican border. There is approximately one agent for every ten miles of the border.

Despite the allocation of personnel, Border Patrol work is frustrating. The U. S.-Mexico border has been called a "never-never land" where the rules don't always apply, where an agent may catch a wetback twice in one night and send him back across the border, only to have him succeed on his third try later the same night. One five-mile stretch, separating suburban San Diego and downtown Tijuana, is a particularly active area. On any single night, 1,000 to 1,500 Mexicans cross the border there. Only 300 to 400 will be caught quickly and returned. A controversial 269-mile fence has been put up, but it is a full-time job just repairing the holes in the fence near San Ysidro, a suburb of San Diego. The fence has been called "the tortilla curtain," a term implying its ineffectiveness.

The Canadian border has recently become more porous as would-be entrants from other nations fly to Toronto or Montreal and then arrange to be smuggled down back roads and across the border. It has always been less heavily patrolled than the Mexican border.

In all aspects of its work, the Border Patrol knows there may never be enough officers to apprehend everyone. There were more than 2,000 border agents in 1979, a 25 percent increase since 1975, but there was also a growing conviction that more border guards will not end illegal immigration. Nor will technology—"sowing the border with more little black boxes that go beep in the night"—stop the human flow. Legislators are looking more to employment sanctions.

As the Border Patrol has become more effective in recent years, those who want to cross a border have looked to smugglers for assistance. In 1974 some 8,073 smugglers and 83,000 smuggled aliens were arrested. In 1979 the numbers had more than doubled to 18,500 smugglers and 211,000 smuggled aliens.

A well-organized smuggling ring stands to make $250,000 a week, or $12 million a year, if it moves 500 aliens a week at $500 apiece. For their fees, the aliens receive little food, water, air, or room to sit. They run the risk of suffocating in airtight vehicles, being thrown from speeding cars, being robbed, beaten, raped, and abandoned in the desert. If anything goes wrong, the smugglers look out for themselves first.

The problems with prosecuting smugglers have been the light sentences they often receive and the difficulty of retaining witnesses to testify against them. Those convicted spend an average of about nineteen months in jail. Smuggling aliens has become more profitable and less risky than smuggling narcotics.

As smuggling increases, so does the potential for violence at the border. In the past, Border Patrol agents have had a gentlemen's agreement with aliens: the agents do not get unnecessarily tough and aliens do not resist when they are caught. But with the growing organization and profitability of smuggling, guns are used more. Bandits from Tijuana also prey on the border-crossers.

Border Patrol agents think something must be done soon to make their jobs performable. "You cannot control the flow of illegal aliens into the United States by any law enforcement method. It's impossible because of sheer numbers," said Chief Patrol Agent Walter Swancutt in El Paso. The Border Patrol can only make it more difficult to come in.

"That border down there is a sieve, and I honestly believe sometimes that if you had Border Patrolmen standing

try are that the workers would use few social services, and the number of workers admitted could be regulated. In recessions and periods of high unemployment, the number admitted would be reduced. The Reagan administration seems to focus on an expanded temporay worker program.

Many European countries have tried "guest workers" programs. Nearly one million Italian workers went to northern Europe to work in 1975, to West Germany, France, the United Kingdom, and Switzerland in particular. Turkey sent 700,000. The experience has not been entirely satisfactory for either side. The workers have contributed to the economic growth of the host countries, but they do not always return to their native countries as planned. When they stay on and marry or bring their families, ethnic tensions rise.

The main opposition to temporary workers comes from organized labor, which sees them as competitors for jobs and as a way to keep wages low. Labor leaders point to what happened in the United States when the bracero program was ended: mechanization took over some jobs, but others were opened up to natives who took them at improved wages. Unemployment for agricultural workers fell from 6.5 percent to 4.8 percent.

A third proposal, often presented along with the employment sanctions or temporary workers program, is an amnesty for the illegal immigrants already settled here. The final report of the Select Commission recommended the legalization of those who had entered the country before January 1, 1980, and had lived here for a period of time to be set by Congress. President Carter had proposed seven consecutive years, a period that would make only about 5 percent of illegal immigrants from Mexico eligible.

The main argument for an amnesty is that massive roundups and deportations of illegal aliens would be inhumane and impractical. The main argument against it is that an amnesty might well encourage others to come illegally.

Other suggestions to curb immigration have included sponsoring development projects in areas of countries that have a large out-migration and encouraging labor-intensive industries to move to countries with large labor pools.

Illegal immigration has become a very sensitive issue between the United States and Mexico. Ruben Bonilla, president of the League of United Latin-American Citizens, says "When you look at Mexico's 30 percent inflation and crippling unemployment, it's clear these people have nowhere else to go. If they couldn't leave, I think social conditions in Mexico could become so bad there would be the loss of the democratic republic in Mexico as we know it." Any United States action against illegal immigrants is bound to have an effect on countries such as Haiti, the Dominican Republic, and El Salvador as well.

Recommendations for Change

Thus, in many respects, United States immigration policy is certainly inconsistent, if not out of control. The job of the Select Commission on Immigration and Refugee Policy was to propose a policy that would be consistent, humane, and enforceable. The task was complicated by the desire of most Americans to continue to welcome immigrants. But most Americans also agree with Father Theodore Hesburgh, chairman of the commission, that "As rich and as large as this nation is, there is no possibility of returning to the virtually unlimited immigration of earlier times."

Some recommendations the commission made are as follows:

1. *How many immigrants shall we admit?* The commis-

sion recommended a modest increase, from 270,000 to 350,000, in the number of legal entrants under the preference system. For the first five years, an additional 100,000 would be admitted to clear up backlogs.

2. *Whom shall we welcome?* The 1965 law has resulted in a heavy emphasis on family reunification. The commission recommends trying to get a broader range of immigrants by establishing a new category for "independents," as described earlier. Some changes were recommended in the family re-unification preferences. The most important was to allow the spouses and children under eighteen of permanent resident aliens to be admitted under a worldwide ceiling instead of under per country limits. This change would ease the situation in countries like Mexico, where the wife or young child of an immigrant may have to wait years to join him.

3. *How can illegal immigration be controlled?* In addition to the amnesty for illegal aliens, the commission recommended better border and interior controls. It backed legislation that would make hiring undocumented workers illegal. Members could not agree, however, to recommend employment identification cards.

The commission presented its recommendations to Congress in 1981, after three years of hearings, studies, and evaluation of testimony. Its work was the first major attempt to overhaul immigration policy since 1911. Whether the recommendations will be implemented is up to Congress and the Reagan administration. The commission included four cabinet officers and eight key members of Congress, but with the change in administration, there may be less consensus on implementing the recommendations. Former Health and Human Services Secretary Patricia Harris predicted that "it will be very difficult to get a new law" but that the commission's work will "provide a plan of action when people are ready for it."

Public opinion seems ready for a more consistent, enforceable policy. As part of its three-year study, the commission invited public comments and received statements like the following:

"It is enticing to play big daddy to all the world's people, but charity begins at home. We have fallen behind in our commitment to our own people."

"People all over the world think that if they don't like things where they are, all they have to do is hop a plane to the United States."

"We have to stop using the stroke-of-a-pen approach to immigration policy."

On the whole, support seems to be growing for a more restrictive immigration policy, but the symbolic transition may be difficult. "A nation steeped in the lore of the Statute of Liberty and the open door will not easily be persuaded that limitation of immigration is in the best interest of all," said a 1980 *Time* essay. But, it added that "rational restriction of immigration is the only recourse for progressive people concerned about the future of mankind."

No matter what the United States decides to do—whether to shoulder an increasing proportion of the world's refugee burden or to draw inward and perfect its own society—the international pressures will continue. Overpopulation, poverty, famine, war, natural disasters, political upheavals will continue to produce emigrants. Commission Chairman Hesburgh predicted that "Large-scale dislocations of people will remain a fact of life for many years to come, not only because most of the world is terribly poor and much of it is not free, but because tens of millions of people see migration as a way to improve their lives."

Modern communication makes Americans more aware of the gap between the rich and the poor, and modern transportation makes the United States more accessible to the strivers in other nations. If this country is to continue to be renewed but not overwhelmed by immigrants, it needs a policy that anticipates the crises of the next twenty-five years. Imagine the scene described by a French novelist, Jean Raspail, in *The Camp of the Saints:* an unarmed invasion fleet of ninety-nine rusting ships carrying nearly a million poor people from Calcutta attempts to land on the French coast. Change the locale to California or Florida and ask, "What should the United States do?"

BIBLIOGRAPHY

Bentley, Judith. *State Government*. American Government Series. New York: Franklin Watts, 1978.
———. *The National Health Care Controversy*. New York: Franklin Watts, 1981.
Bryce-Laporte, Roy Simon. *Sourcebook on the New Immigration*. New Brunswick, N. J.: Transaction Books, 1980.
Castro, Tony. *Chicano Power: The Emergence of Mexican America*. New York: Saturday Review Press-E. P. Dutton, 1974.
Chaney, Elsa M., and Sutton, Constance L., eds. "Caribbean Migration to New York." *International Migration Review* (Summer 1979), 13:2.
Congressional Research Service. *U. S. Immigration Law and Policy, 1952-1979*. Washington, D. C.: Government Printing Office, 1979.
Ehrlich, Paul R.; Bilderback, Loy; and Ehrlich, Anne H. *The Golden Door: International Migration, Mexico and the United*

States. New York: Ballantine, 1979.

Halsell, Grace. *The Illegals.* New York: Stein & Day, 1978.

"Hispanic Americans: Soon the Biggest Minority." *Time,* October 16, 1978, pp. 48–52.

Melendy, H. Brett. *Asians in America: Filipinos, Koreans, and East Indians.* Boston: Twayne, 1977.

"Special issue on Haitians." *Migration Today* (September 1979), 7:4 (Center for Migration Studies, 209 Flagg Place, Staten Island, N. Y. 10304).

"The New Immigrants," *Newsweek,* July 7, 1980, pp. 26–31.

Rice, William T.; Lamanna, Maryanne; and Murata, Alice. *Transition to Nowhere: Vietnamese Refugees in America.* Nashville: Charter House, 1979.

Tanton, John. *Rethinking Immigration Policy: America in the 1980s—Meeting the Challenge of Legal and Illegal Immigration.* Washington, D. C.: Federation for American Immigration Reform, 1980.

U. S. Immigration Policy and the National Interest, The Final Report and Recommendations of the Select Commission on Immigration and Refugee Policy. Washington, D. C.: Government Printing Office, March 1, 1981.

INDEX

187

Philippines (Filipinos), 11–12, 18,
61, 62, 64–69, 125, 128, 139,
142
Physicians, 127–28. *See also*
Brain drain; specific groups
Point system, 169
Poles, 117, 119, 151
Political refugees. *See* Refugees
Politics, 136–41
Population pressure, 23, 163–64
Portugal; Portuguese, 111–15, 133
Preference system, 20, 169–70
Professional and technical jobs,
126, 127–28. *See also* Brain
drain; specific groups
Puerto Ricans, 34, 48–50, 58, 59,
137, 144
Push-pull factors, 22–24

Reagan administration, 179, 181
Refugee Act of 1980, 85, 118, 166
Refugees, 131, 132–33, 165–68.
See also specific groups
Relatives, 170–72
Religion, 134–35. *See also* specific groups
Rivers, Norma Beckles, 12, 95
Rumanians, 117
Russians, 110, 117–19, 137

Salvadoreans. *See* El Salvador
Samoans, 62
San Antonio, Texas, 40, 138
San Diego, 90, 175
San Francisco, 55, 69, 75, 77–78
Santa Anna, Antonio López de, 40
Santo Domingo, 51, 52
San Ysidro, Calif., 114, 175
Seadrift, Texas, 89–90
Seattle, 69, 139
Select Commission on Immigration and Refugee Policy, 31,
161–62ff., 180–82

Serbo-Croatians, 137
Sheater, Colleen, 87
Sikh religion, 80
Social services, 155–57
South Americans, 35, 53, 55–56
Southeast Asians, 82–90. *See also*
specific groups
Soviet Jews. *See* Jews

Tai Dam, the, 89
Taiwan, 73
Tampa, 58
Teamsters' union, 67
Temporary-worker program,
178–79
Texas, 30, 34, 40, 41, 58, 85,
89–90, 91, 126, 136, 138, 139,
156
Thailand; Thais, 61, 62
Tijuana, 40, 175, 176
Tobago, 93, 94, 103, 104
Trinidad, 93, 94, 103ff.

Union City, N.J., 45
Unions, 154–55

Vietnamese, 1, 6, 28, 62, 82–90,
112, 127, 132, 135, 140
Visas, 21, 148

Washington, D.C., 68, 70, 90, 151
Watts, Calif., 140
Wealthy, the, 121
Weatherford, Ark., 90
Welfare, 129, 157
West Indians. *See* Caribbean islanders
Women, 129, 133
World War I, 16–17
World War II, 17–18, 62

Young Lords, 40
Yugoslavia, 137

About the Author

Judith Bentley is a graduate of Oberlin College and holds a master's degree in the History of American Civilization from New York University. She is a freelance writer and the author of *State Government* and *The National Health Care Controversy*. Ms. Bentley lives with her husband and two small children in Washington state. While writing this book, she lived in Brooklyn and within walking distance were a Korean fruit and vegetable stand, a Lebanese restaurant, an Italian butcher, the West Indian annual festival, a Vietnamese restaurant, numerous Puerto Rican bodegas, and an occasional fireworks display over the Statue of Liberty.